The Buchanans of 1790

James Buchanan

HERITAGE BOOKS
2014

HERITAGE BOOKS
AN IMPRINT OF HERITAGE BOOKS, INC.

Books, CDs, and more—Worldwide

For our listing of thousands of titles see our website
at
www.HeritageBooks.com

Published 2014 by
HERITAGE BOOKS, INC.
Publishing Division
5810 Ruatan Street
Berwyn Heights, Md. 20740

Heritage Books by the author:
The Blacks of Pickaway County, Ohio in the Nineteenth Century
The Buchanans of 1790

International Standard Book Numbers
Paperbound: 978-0-7884-5593-3
Clothbound: 978-0-7884-6050-0

For Sgt. David A. Buchanan, U.S.M.C.
January 1951 – December 2007

TABLE OF CONTENTS

INTRODUCTION

The young nation was taking its first census of its residents in 1790. Among the various people were large numbers of Scottish and Scotch-Irish families. Of these, one family would become better known in the 1800s when one of its members would be president - that of the Buchanans. This book looks at the Buchanan families of the United States in 1790.

When the census was taken in August 1790, it was limited to the 13 states and the district of Maine. Arrangements were made for other districts that were not yet part of the United States. Kentucky's census was taken the week after it broke off from Virginia to begin the process of seeking statehood. The Southwest Territory, as Tennessee was known at that time, had a count done of the number of inhabitants but no names were recorded. The census of Vermont was taken immediately after it became a state in 1791.

The major problem with the 1790 census came about not because of delays in counting, but the War of 1812. In August 1814, census records that were stored in the State Department in Washington, D.C. were burned by the British when they sacked the city and burned government buildings. Some argue that as a result, the census records for several areas were lost for the years 1790 to 1810, although some states maintained copies of the later years so that the only loss was the 1790 census data. These sources say that the records of Delaware, Georgia, Kentucky, New Jersey, Tennessee and Virginia were all burned. There were Buchanan families in each of these areas, so they are not listed in the "official" census that remains.

Other sources indicate a different reason for the lost records. The law requiring the census indicated that the records were to be stored with the clerk of the district courts in the states and the census records were not consolidated in Washington, D.C. until 1830. The records that burned were only the statistical totals, not the individual records. Accordingly, some of the census records were somehow lost in the various states rather than destroyed by the British. This might also explain the problems in the Trans-Appalachian districts as they were not yet states with district courts for filing the census records.

Regardless of the reason, it is clear that some state and district records were burned or lost and they are no longer available. For this reason, the census had to be reconstructed using alternate records available for the period around 1790. To examine the 1790 population beyond statistical totals requires that one look at local records or summaries of other data as close in time as possible. For example, in Virginia, Augusta Fothergill's list of Virginia taxpayers from 1782-1787 provides a substantial record of the families a short time before the census. Some state censuses from, 1787 through 1792 provide further data. Fairly close in time personal and real property tax records, deeds, estate records and local histories are available for the states and districts in which records were lost or destroyed.

So who were these Buchanans in the new nation? The official census lists more than 150 families with twenty-one different spelling variations for the name. Among the families were 740 white individuals, four black freedmen and 219 slaves. Interestingly, one black freedman owned slaves. The reconstructed records and local sources add many more families and slaves to the story, especially in the areas where no official "census" records remain.

Most of the Buchanans were farmers, as were most Americans of the time. Occupationally, merchants were the second most represented occupation among the families. Many of the white adult males and at least one black freedman had served in the Revolutionary War. Most of the parents were foreign-born while about half of the children were first-generation Americans. Scotch-Irish birth was more prevalent due both to the earlier migration of many Scottish families who had fled to Ireland before coming to the United States, but also the departure of Loyalists of Scottish birth from the United States after the Revolutionary War.

As the nation was sectionalized at the time, this book will also look at the Buchanans in the various sections of the nation. Among the states and districts, all had Buchanan families listed except for the New England states and districts, Vermont being the only exception to the rule. As with the overall population, many traits were regionalized so that Vermont Buchanan families had different traits from the middle state families, and southern Buchanans were different from both. Among the southern states, the upper south states of Maryland and Virginia had the most slave-holding Buchanan families as opposed to the deep southern states. Finally, the frontier areas which were not yet states had families more concerned with survival on the frontier than being counted with those on the coast.

The information included for many of the heads of household comes mostly from local sources. A number of persons have no information included because none could be found in available local resources. Only a small amount of information is included from genealogical sources. The biggest reason for limiting this type of information is that there are often differences in the same family line being compiled by different people. In addition, the Buchanans were unfortunate to be the subject of the Buchanan Scam in the 1930s when genealogies were altered by thousands seeking a share of a supposed fortune that didn't exist.

There is also a warning that accompanies all genealogical work. Applying what Ronald Reagan used to say, one needs to test and verify the data. This is true of any genealogical data, including that in this book. An example of the potential problems with genealogical data can be found in some areas such as Augusta, Washington and Wythe Counties in Virginia where there were numerous Buchanans of the same given name. Trying to match local data to specific persons is difficult at best and impossible at worst. In such cases that data has been matched to the head of households where possible and comments are made after listing two or more persons of the same name when it is not possible. In matching data, one can find, for example, that a single man did not have a large family in 1790 so the listed head of household with large families would probably not be the person to which the data refers. Where local sources mention additional persons of the same name, these are added for each county after the discussion of the heads of households cited in the federal or reconstructed censuses.

Also, the census takers of 1790 spelled the name differently and at least nineteen different spellings of Buchanan appear in the records. Many of the spellings would change in the subsequent censuses. But for the purposes of 1790 they are listed by their original spellings. Despite all of the shortcomings of the census, in the end this book tries to sort out the data and identify families based on the best data discovered.

Finally, this book is not intended to be a complete genealogy of any family, but some information is included where it was located. Rather, the concept is to show the geographic distribution and movement of Buchanan families in a static slice of time correlating to the years in close proximity to the first census of the United States. As with any other genealogical work, the reader is encouraged to dig deeper and look at other sources to determine the best information for those who came before them.

Chapter One

NEW ENGLAND

The United States of 1790 was far different than the country we know today. Even in the settled sections of the country, not all were settled within states that had been admitted to the Union. New England consisted of only four states in 1790, those being Connecticut, Massachusetts, New Hampshire and Rhode Island. Maine would not be formed from Massachusetts for another 30 years. Vermont existed theoretically as part of New York but in reality as an independent entity awaiting statehood. Nevertheless, Vermont was eventually included in the census of 1790, although there were gaps in the count.

Vermont

In New England there were Buchanan families in only one area, that being eastern Vermont. This land had been claimed previously by Massachusetts, New Hampshire and New York. Prior to the end of the French and Indian Wars in 1763, Massachusetts held what was, in reality, a paper claim based on an old charter. Being contiguous claimants, New Hampshire and New York both made land grants to the lands west of the Green Mountains and Connecticut River. These claims often overlapped, causing conflict between those trying to settle based on their particular grant. The result was conflict and violence between the parties.

To resolve the conflict, King George supposedly settled the legal claims in a 1764 charter declaring the New Hampshire border with New York along the Connecticut River. But establishing the border on paper did not resolve the problem as Ethan Allen and the militia called the Green Mountain Boys drove out the New Yorkers in favor of the New Hampshire grantees. Once the Revolution began, it was Allen and his troops, which essentially served as the local militia of the region. In that capacity, Allen and his Green Mountain Boys captured Fort

Ticonderoga and delivered the fort's cannons to George Washington as part of the action to drive the British out of Boston.

With the Revolution in full swing, a convention of Vermonters met on January 15, 1777 and declared the territory an independent region. Historian Frederic Van De Water indicates that the territory was named the Republic of New Connecticut until June 1777 when it took on the name Vermont, which is French for "Green Mountains".

On July 1, 1777, the convention enacted the first written constitution for an independent state in North America, creating the Republic of Vermont. The verbiage was mixed as the Constitution also referred to Vermont as the "State of Vermont" and a Commonwealth. As part of that Constitution, slavery was abolished. For that reason, there were no slaves to report in Vermont during the 1790 census, while Connecticut, New Hampshire and Massachusetts all reported slaves in their states at that time.

The next year the first General Assembly was held in Vermont. The Republic acted independently of the American colonists during the War, even to the point of negotiating with the British about becoming part of Canada. Vermont also coined its own currency and operated its own postal system. Yet the underlying desire of the citizenry was reflected in the coinage and official documents which used the term "State of Vermont."

In the end, the majority were granted their wish to be part of the United States. After the Revolutionary War, New York's objections prevented statehood for Vermont for several years. But on March 4, 1791, Vermont became the 14th state of the United States and a month later the official "1790" census was taken of the state.

Among the settlers of Vermont prior to any of these events happening were some Scots who had served as soldiers in the French and Indian Wars and who remained in New England after the war. These early residents settled predominantly along the west side of the Connecticut River and its tributaries. They were joined in the following years by Scottish immigrants who came to Vermont and settled mainly in the same areas along the Connecticut River. When counties were created in Vermont, one of the two counties was named Orange in honor of the Scottish population. All of the Scottish settlements in Vermont at that time were located within Orange County. The year after the census was taken, this county was split, Caledonia County was created from Orange County and both counties were named for the Scottish heritage of the local population. For purposes of the 1791 census, all of the Buchanans were within the boundaries of Orange County, although some were in the area that was split off and became Caledonia County after the census was taken.

Into Vermont came Scottish immigrants. Located in Orange County, Barnet was first settled beginning in 1763, but later became part of Caledonia County. Ryegate was begun in 1773 and Chelsea in 1781, both of which remain in Orange County today. Most of the Buchanans in these areas came in 1784 when a large number of Scots left their homes and came to the new territory once the Treaty of Paris was signed and peace returned to America.

Many of the Scots who came to America in this period were sponsored by immigration companies formed in Scotland. The best-documented Vermont example of this is found in the example of Ryegate, settled by the Scots-American Company of Ryegate. James Whitelaw and David Allan, as commissioners of the Company, purchased the south half of the town in 1773 and immigrants began arriving to claim lots there in 1774. The immigrants that were convinced to leave their homes in Scotland and settle in Orange County were mainly farmers and craftsmen.

Unlike in many areas of New England, the Scotch-Irish were not among these early settlers. They had come into New England early in the 1700s and had formed cities such as Londonderry and Derry, New Hampshire and Worcester,

3

Massachusetts. This was a variation from the normal settlement pattern in other states where the Scotch-Irish settled on the western frontier, and the Scots on the coast. But in Vermont it was generally the Scottish-born that came to live further west than the Scotch-Irish in Massachusetts and New Hampshire.

Buchanans in Vermont, 1790

Only two Buchanan families are listed in the Vermont census of 1791 as recognized by the U.S. Census Bureau. These are:

Orange County - Barnet
John Buchanan - three white males over age 16, one under 16, four white females.

John Buchanan was born in 1744 in Buchanan Parish, Scotland. He lived in Glasgow and Paisley, Scotland before coming to America in 1785 with his wife, Ann (Campbell) and their six children. After two or three years in Hempstead, New Hampshire, he moved to Barnet. At the time of the census, the children included Ann, Archibald, Elizabeth, Janet, John and Mabel. John died in 1831 and Ann in 1817.

Orange County - Chelsea
Stephen Buckannan - one white male over age 16, two under 16, two white females

Thus the official "1790" Vermont census reports two Buchanan families comprised of 13 people, with no freedmen or slaves. This was not surprising because slavery was illegal in Vermont and the black population of the state was negligible.

But the story of the Buchanans in 1790 Vermont does not end there. One has to look at local histories to find other families, and even these additions may not be complete.

The "History of the Town of Barnet"[1] includes other Buchanan families that came in 1784. **James Buchanan** was born in 1772 in Drummond Parish, Stirlingshire, Scotland, a son of Peter and Annabel (Miller) Buchanan. He migrated from Stirlingshire, Scotland as did his brothers Henry, Alexander, and Peter Buchanan. Three times during the 1780s he was a signatory to petitions in Barnet and he took the Freeman's Oath of Allegiance in Barnet on March 11, 1785.

While James was in America in 1790, it is uncertain about the other brothers. When Alexander (born 1771) actually arrived in Vermont is a question mark, as neither he nor James is found in the 1790 census, but both are in the 1800 census. Despite being missed in the official federal census, James Buchanan is listed in the reconstructed Vermont census of 1791. As for the other family members, both Henry and Peter Buchanan immigrated to Vermont in 1806 with their parents after James returned to Scotland and brought them to America.

Although the evidence points to the fact that James Buchanan was a Barnet resident in 1790, yet another local history book indicates otherwise. The History of Newbury, Vermont[2] claims James was a resident of New Hampshire at the time. The Newbury history agrees with the Scottish portion of James' life but says he came to America and settled in New Hampshire in 1785, working as a wheelwright in Maine. Some of the confusion may come because he did marry Elizabeth (Hurd) in Rochester, New Hampshire, in 1790 as that book indicates. But that does not mean that he was a resident of New Hampshire at that time. No Buchanans are identified in the 1790 New Hampshire census, and the other evidence, such as the Barnet petitions and Freedman's Oath, indicate that James Buchanan was in Vermont rather than New Hampshire.

James and Elizabeth had eleven children after the 1790 census. In 1806 he returned to Scotland and brought the remainder of his family, including his parents and brothers Henry and Peter. Both James and Elizabeth are found in the Barnet

Center Cemetery today, James passing away in 1831 and Elizabeth in 1842.

Alexander, whose arrival date is uncertain, married Martha (Moore) in 1801 and had eight children. He died in 1853. Two of his children moved to Iowa and one to Massachusetts.

The reconstructed records of 1791 Vermont did not always match what is listed in the federal census. As listed in the Ancestry.com compiled census substitutes index, the Vermont state census in 1791 included **Ananiah Buchanan** in Chelsea as well as Stephen, the latter listed in the official census. There may be some confusion with this Buchanan because there are no other sources in the time period that place Ananiah in Vermont, but there are sources listing an Ananiah Bohannon/Bohonon in New Hampshire in 1790. He moved to Vermont in 1807. Why he was listed in the 1791 Vermont census but also New Hampshire records in 1790 is unknown.

Bohannon is the variation of Buchanan that came from Northern Ireland after the Scottish refugees settled there in the 1700s, so it is possible that the man changed his name back to Buchanan as others did in the southern states. This is probably the case here because he was registered as Ananiah Buchanan, a Private in the New Hampshire Militia, then a Lieutenant and Captain of Continental troops during the Revolution.

So in 1791 Vermont, there were at least as many Buchanan families not listed as those who were listed. It is hard to determine the total, not knowing how many of those in Barnet were living independently or whether there were others not visible in local records. One thing is clear, however, and that is that there were other Buchanans beyond those counted by the census takers.

[1]"History of the Town of Barnet," in Hamilton Child, *Gazetteer of Caledonia and Essex Counties, VT, 1764-1887* (Author, May 1887), 133, 151.

[2]Frederic P. Wells, *History of Newbury, Vermont, 1704-1902* (St. Johnsbury, Vermont: Caledonian Co., 1902), 481-482.

Chapter Two

MIDDLE STATES

The area of greatest international competition for colonies in North America in the 1600s was in the area of the Middle Colonies. From Spain's initial exploration to the British seizure of most of the land in 1664, these colonies were a battleground between nations. Dutch settlement came first, followed by Swedes and Finns, and then the British seized all of these future states in 1664.

By 1790, these states were growing numerically but differing in economic base. New York was building a future commercial capital of America, while Pennsylvania was the frontier state where farming was king and religious freedom attracted various sects from Europe, especially the Germanic areas. New Jersey was split between coastal commercialism and inland agriculture. Delaware remained the smallest of the states, under Pennsylvania's indirect rule.

New York

The growing commercial giant began as a small Dutch settlement called New Netherlands. Henry Hudson had explored the River which bore his name as an employee of the Dutch East India Company. Although looking for a Northwest Passage to the East, he laid the foundation of Dutch settlement in 1609.

The Dutch East India Company established a trading post in what is now New York City in 1624. The next year came the infamous Manhattan Purchase when the Dutch purchased the area of modern New York from the Indians. In 1626 a fort was built and settlers arrived. Slaves were imported to help with building and defense of the city. The city was chartered as New Amsterdam in 1653, then in 1664 the English defeated the Dutch in both the northern (New York, New Jersey, Connecticut) and southern (Delaware) areas, renaming the northern land after the Duke of York, hence New York.

In the meantime, smaller Dutch settlements had been established along the Hudson River all the way to modern Albany, which was settled in 1614 but not chartered until 1684 after the British took control. Additional settlements were opened in New Jersey, Delaware and modern Hartford, Connecticut.

New York was commercially split between inland areas and the area surrounding Manhattan. The river valleys provided agricultural lands for both large plantation-type estates and small farms. Fur trading by the French in the north and the English in the south produced resources to export. Industry was concentrated mainly in the New York City area and was aimed at furnishing products to export to the Old World.

New York City provided the commercial hub for the colony, later state of New York. From docks to warehouses, the port developed quickly. Whether farm goods, furs or commercial products made by local artisans, the point of transit was New York City. Many of the slaves in New York were located in the City as well, making up 25% of the entire population in 1684, but declining to 16% of the population in 1720, and continuing to be reduced as a total percentage of the population after that date.

As in many of the colonies, there were differing time periods and areas of interest for immigrants from Scotland and those from Ireland of Scottish heritage. The Scotch-Irish came first, in the early and mid-1700s. They came as Irishmen of Scottish blood, their descendants having fled Scotland in the homeland wars from the mid-1600s to mid-1700s, many using the city as a transit point to other areas in New England and further South. For those who stayed, the Scotch-Irish settled in areas near New York City. Ulster County, named after the homeland, was one of the original British counties of New York in 1683. Scotch-Irish settlement occurred in both the part of the county that would remain Ulster County but also that part which would later become part of Orange County.

The Scottish settlers to New York tended to come later in the 18th century. When they arrived, they settled in either New York City or upstate, depending on their economic situation. Merchants tended to stay in New York City while farmers moved inland. Some Highland troops stayed after the French and Indian Wars, often seeking land in areas which they had seen or where they had fought during the war. Closer in time to the Revolution, Sir William Johnson convinced immigrant Scots to settle in the Mohawk Valley.

When war came, the allegiances of the Scottish-Americans split along lines reflecting their heritage. Scottish immigrants generally remained loyal to the Crown and two Scottish-American regiments were formed to fight for the British. Scotch-Irish settlers generally fought for the colonies against their brethren. After the Revolution, a great percentage of the Loyalists, especially those in New York City, left for resettlement in Canada. New York Buchanans who served in the American forces during the Revolution included Ebenezer and Patrick Buchanan (Albany), James Buchanan (Orange County), William Buchanan (Suffolk County), Robert Buchanan (Ulster County) and John and Samuel Buchanan of the New York State Line.

By 1790, the population of New York had grown to 340,120. The percentage of slaves continued to drop, and by 1790 was less than 10% of the population. While slaves numbered 21,193 in New York in 1790, it was one of the urban centers which sheltered free blacks as well.

Buchanans in 1790 New York

Numerous Buchanans appear in the earlier colonial history of New York as well as in the census rolls of 1790. Scotch-Irish Buchanan families settled in Ulster County during the migration period and their families remained in the new country. In New

11

York City, Scottish merchants such as Thomas and Walter Buchanan remained. In fact, these Buchanans owned large amounts of property, including part of Wall Street. In the 1930s, as various scandals swirled around supposed heirs of a vast Buchanan estate left by a member of President James Buchanan's family or the President himself. One of those whose name surfaced as an alternative to the President was Thomas Buchanan who supposedly left hundreds of millions of dollars for heirs.

The Buchanan merchants owned slaves in 1790. Thomas Buchanan had six slaves while Walter Buchanan had four slaves. In Ulster County, John Buchanan owned three slaves. There is no indication whether these slaves were for domestic or business service, but may have included both.

New York State was one of two states with free black persons with the family name Buchanan. A free black person lived in the home of William Buchanan in New York City. Because no age or gender is provided in the census for free persons of other color, little more is known from the census records.

Albany – Cambridge –
Patrick Buchannon – two white males over 16, two under 16, three females

Patrick Buchannon lived in Albany County in 1776 and served in the 16th Regiment of Albany County Militia in the Revolutionary War. He was on the tax lists of Cambridge Township in Albany County. In 1791 Cambridge became part of Washington County.

Although not in the official census, there was a **Thomas Buchanan** resident of Cambridge at least a small part of 1790 with a wife and one child.

Thomas Buchanan was born in 1767 in County Donegal, Ireland, the son of John and Jane (Russell) Buchanan. He came to

12

America where he married Sarah (Livingston) in Oneida, New York in 1791. Their first child, Elizabeth, was born in 1790 either in Ireland, at sea on the way to America, or in Cambridge, depending on the source. After settling in Cambridge, which was taken from Albany County and put in the newly-created Washington County in 1791, their second child was born in December 1791 in Cambridge. The couple had seven children. Later the family moved to Cattaraugus County where Sarah died in 1843 and Thomas died in 1853. Both are buried in the Napoli Cemetery in Cattaraugus County.

New York City – East Ward
   Thomas Buchanan – two white males over 16, nine females, six slaves

   As a successful businessman, Thomas Buchanan was one of the better-known Buchanans in 1790 New York. Born to George and Jean (Lowden) Buchanan in Glasgow, Scotland in December 1744, he studied at the University of Glasgow, graduating in 1762. The next year he left Scotland for New York in 1763 and developed a mercantile business with a cousin of his father, Walter Buchanan, who was already a New York merchant. By 1765 the business was the largest commercial operation in terms of the most ships owned in New York City. Eventually the partners changed as Walter Buchanan retired from the firm and Thomas added a brother and later his son to the firm.

   Walter and Thomas Buchanan traded both domestically and with foreign nations prior to the war and Thomas remained neutral during the Revolutionary War, walking both sides of a fine line in his attempt to remain neutral. He returned a load of tea to Britain in 1774 but along with most New York merchants signed a loyalty address to the king in 1776. During the Revolution, Thomas served on the governing body of New York City, as well as an officer of the Chamber of Commerce. He was noted for his kindness to American prisoners of war in New York City. Yet Thomas owned six slaves which tarnishes the humanitarian aspects of his legacy.

Following the war, Thomas Buchanan was an Associate Director of the U.S. Bank. He died in November 1815. It was said that he was one of the richest and most influential New York merchants both before and after the Revolutionary War.

Thomas Buchanan married Ann (Townsend) at Oyster Bay in 1765 and had several children. They had a home on Wall Street in New York, prior to its becoming the financial center of the country.

William Buckanan – two white males over 16, one female, one free black person

William Buchanan – one white male over 16, one female

It is difficult to decide which William Buchanan was which in the context of available information. One of the William Buchanans was a doctor in New York City. One married Ann (McCulloch) and had children baptized at the First Presbyterian Church of New York in 1791 and 1792.

One William Buchanan had a dry goods company, William Buchanan & Co. which dissolved in 1793. He was found on the tax list in 1791 but in 1796 his business burned and in 1798 his name appeared on the list of paupers. In January 1799 he returned to Glasgow, Scotland.

New York City - Montgomery Ward
John Buchanan – one white male over 16, one under 16, four females

John Buchanan was a New York grocer who married Ann (Luce) and had children Annie, Catherine, George and Polly listed in his will. She inherited several houses from her father in 1793, John being the executor of the estate. John died in 1812 in New York City and Ann was the administratrix of his estate.

Sally Buchanan – single white female

Walter Buchanan – one white male over 16, three under 16, three females, four slaves

The other half of the business partnership of Thomas and Walter Buchanan, the elder Walter Buchanan was already operating a mercantile business when Thomas arrived in New York. Born to Alexander Buchanan in Glasgow, Walter was a cousin of Thomas Buchanan's father. When the younger Buchanan arrived in 1763, the two formed a partnership which lasted until 1772.

When the war came to New York City in 1777, Walter Buchanan moved to Hanover, New Jersey, where he remained until the end of the war. Returning to New York, he formed the firm of Buchanan & Thomson which lasted from 1784 to 1787. After 1787, Walter Buchanan operated his own dry goods business.

Walter Buchanan m. Lillias (Campbell) in 1769. The couple had four children, three of whom died young. Their son, Walter, Jr., became a doctor of note in New York. Walter Buchanan died and was buried in Schenectady, New York in 1815.

One of only three New York Buchanans who owned slaves, Walter had four.

In addition to those listed in New York City for the 1790 census, there was also a **James Buchanan**, Esquire who was listed as a male head of household in the New York City Directory of 1786 and was the director of a bank in New York City. He may still have been in New York City at the time of the census, although this is uncertain.

Similarly, there was a **David Buchanan** listed in records as living in New York City in 1776 and 1781. He married Mary

(Connell), a widow, on May 19, 1778. Whether he was still in New York City in 1790 is unknown.

Queens
William Buchanan –one white male over 16, two under 16, two females

William Buchanan was still listed in the county with a family of four in 1800.

Richmond
George Buchannan – one white male over 16, one under 16, four females

George Buchannan lived in Westfield Township.

Ulster County – Montgomery
William Buchanan – one white male over 16, one under 16, three females

There is a difference of information on William Buchanan, depending on the source of the information. It appears that he was born in Scotland sometime between the 1730s and 1750. He moved from Perthshire, Scotland to America in 1786. In 1777, William married Janet (Kinder) (born 1755, died 1817, Montgomery County. New York). The couple had four children, one of whom, Alexander, was born prior to the census. The children later moved to Alabama and Texas. William died and was buried in Orange County in 1802 after that part of Ulster County was incorporated into Orange County.

Although not in the census records, another **William Buchanan** appears in Montgomery, in 1790. William Buchanan was born in 1759 in Orange County, the son of James Buchanan,. He married Susannah (Bodine) (born 1761, died 1819, Montgomery, Orange County) and had four children baptized at the Brick Reformed Church of Montgomery, Orange County, New

16

York between 1789 and 1792. Only Mary was born prior to the census. William Buchanan died in 1842 in Blooming Grove, Orange County.

Ulster County – New Windsor

James Buchanan I – one white male over 16, two under 16, one female

James was the son of Robert and Elizabeth (Falls) Buchanan. He married Elizabeth (Galloway) and settled in Haverstraw, New York, which became part of Rockland County after it was separated from Orange County in 1798. He is listed in the New Windsor census of 1775.

James Buchanan, II – one white male over 16, one under 16, three females

James Buchanan II was in the area that became part of Orange County in 1798 and is listed in the 1800 census there with a family of seven.

John Buchanan – one white male over 16, three under 16, two females, one slave

John Buchanan was born prior to 1760 in Little Britain, Orange County, New York, a son of James Buchanan. He served as a Private in the New York Militia and as a member of the 2nd Artillery company of the Continental Army during the Revolutionary War. He was also ordered into service for the defense of West Point. He married Miriam (Eager) and had several children, Thomas and James being born before the census. After this, he settled in Herkimer County in the Mohawk Valley of New York. He is listed in the 1800 census with a family of eight and one slave. John Buchanan died in Herkimer in either 1806 or 1808.

Also in New Windsor, Ulster County were other Buchanans who are found in local records and may have been living in the county in 1790. Most of these are the children of Robert and Elizabeth (Falls) Buchanan or James Buchanan. These include **Arthur Buchanan**, **George Buchanan**, another **James Buchanan**, two **Robert Buchanans**, and a **Samuel Buchanan**.

Arthur Buchanan was born in 1766 in Orange County, the son of Robert and Elizabeth (Falls) Buchanan. He lived in Walkill, Orange County and was a witness to a will in 1789.

George Buchanan was born in Orange County in 1763, the son of Robert and Elizabeth (Falls) Buchanan. He may have been living with his parents in 1790 as he did not marry Sarah (Eldred) until 1795. He died in 1847.

James Buchanan, son of James Buchanan, was born in 1761 in Orange County. He married Martha (Eager) (born 1746, died 1795) in 1790 at the First Presbyterian Church of Goshen, New York. The couple had no children.

Born in Scotland in 1729, **Robert Buchanan** was the son of Robert and Catherine (McDonnell) Buchanan. He served in the Albany County Militia in the Revolution. Robert married Elizabeth (Falls) in 1755 and the couple had ten children. He later moved to Pennsylvania where he died in 1818.

The other **Robert Buchanan** was born in 1766 in Orange County, son of James Buchanan. He married Hannah (Campbell) and died in 1809. It is possible that he was living as a single man with his parents in 1790.

Samuel Buchanan witnessed a will and a codicil in November 1787. Samuel may have been the man who served in the 2nd New York Line during the Revolutionary War.

New Jersey

Colonial New Jersey began as a zone in which various nations made settlements in the early and mid-1600s. Unlike in New York and Delaware, these various nationalities were generally allowed to live peacefully together and not be involved in struggles between nations.

Dutch settlement began in 1624 under Cornelius May for which modern Cape May is named. Dutch, Swedes and Finns all settled in the state and lived peacefully. The first city charter was grated to Bergen in 1661. The British takeover became official in 1674 and the colony was renamed New Jersey. At that time a proprietorship was established which reflected the divided colony. Economically coastal settlers engaged in fishing and commerce while inland settlers were generally farmers. Politically, the colony was divided with an even number of English and Scottish proprietors. Recognizing this split, the coastal areas of the eastern shore were considered to be Scottish and the western inland side of the colony was English.

In 1702 the divided colony was united under British control. But the history of division did not resolve itself through the 18th century. When war came, many loyalists and freed slaves fought for the British, while the people in the inland areas were more likely to support the American forces. Several Loyalist units were raised in New Jersey and fought against the American forces. Even Benjamin Franklin's family was split as he served the forces of freedom while his son was the Loyalist governor of New Jersey. Many of the battles of the Revolution were also fought in New Jersey.

Scottish involvement in New Jersey came because of the proprietorship arrangement. Cities such as Perth Amboy were established by Scots. Scots came as immigrant merchants or indentured servants. An estimated half of the Scottish immigrants came either as indentured servants or prisoners of war from the wars between Scotland and England in the 1700s. Unlike neighboring New York and Pennsylvania, New Jersey did not experience a large influx of Scotch-Irish as the major ports of such immigration were New York and Philadelphia.

The Census Bureau estimated that the population of New Jersey in 1790 was 184,139, with a slave population of 11,423. But the 1790 census records for the state were either burned or lost. As a result, records such as a state census and the reconstructed census records are the source of the information from New Jersey. Stryker-Rodda's Revolutionary Census of New Jersey[1] looks at the residents between 1773 and 1784. Ancestry.com's Reconstructed Census looks at what they believe existed in 1790 using local records or possibly using the state militia rolls of 1793.

Buchanans of New Jersey, 1790

The heads of household listed here are from the Reconstructed Census records for New Jersey. Many are based on petition signatures from residents of various counties while others come from tax lists or other data from the years around 1790. Most do not list family composition, only the head of the household. These petitions may be found in the New Jersey State Archives Collection.

Burlington County
    Samuel Buchanan

Samuel Buchanan is counted in the 1790 substitute census because of his signature as a county resident on a 1790 petition to the Legislative Council and General Assembly. He served as a Private of New Jersey troops during the Revolution.

Thomas Buchanan

Thomas Buchanan was counted in the 1790 substitute census because of his signatures as a county resident on a 1790 petition to the Legislative Council and General Assembly.

Burlington County – Burlington Township
Abraham Buchanan
John Buchanan

Abraham and John Buchanan are counted in the substitute census because of their signatures on a petition to the state Legislative Council.

Cumberland County
James Buchanan

Michel Buchanan

Michel Buchanan was included in the substitute census because of a variety of court petitions to the "inferior" judges of the Court of Common Pleas during the 1780s-1790s.

Nathan Buchanan

As with Michel Buchanan, Nathan Buchanan signed as a resident a petition requesting a road in the county.

Essex County – Elizabeth Township
William Buchanan

William Buchanan signed a 1791 petition from citizens of Trenton to the state Legislative Council.

Gloucester County
Cornelius Buchanan

Cornelius Buchanan is counted in the substitute census because of his signature on a 1790 petition to the Legislative Council and General Assembly. The signature appears as "Corns" but he is listed as Cornelius. He had also signed petitions as a resident in 1786.

Joseph Buchanan

Joseph Buchanan was included in the substitute census because of his signature as a resident on petitions to the state Legislative Council in the early 1790s

Hunterdon County, Amwell Township
John Buchanan

John Buchanan was born about 1740. He owned Buchanan's Tavern in Hunterdon County. At the time of his death in 1818, he was married with nine children and two slaves according to his will. He had at least one son, Archibald, born in 1790.

Hunterdon County - Trenton
Th? Buchanan

Although the full name of this Buchanan is not listed, he served as a Lieutenant of an Infantry Company in Hunterdon County in 1787.

Morris County – Hanover Township
Walter Buchanan – wife, daughter

Walter Buchanan appears in both Stryker-Rodda's Revolutionary War census and in the substitute 1790 census for New Jersey as well as county and church records throughout the

1780s. In 1790 was married with at least one daughter, born in 1780. He may also have been the man named Arthur who served as an Artificer in the Quartermaster Corps of New Jersey during the Revolutionary War.

Salem County – Elsinboro Township
John Buchanan

John Buchanan was noted in the substitute census index because of his signature on petitions to the state legislative council and General Assembly in the early 1790s.

Salem County, Pikegrove Township
James Buchanan - wife, son

At the time of the 1790 census, James Buchanan was married with at least one son who was born in 1780. He moved to Kentucky by 1805 and then to Missouri.

Sussex County – James Bucanan
Robert Bucanan
Robert Bucanan

Two Robert Bucanans are listed in Sussex County in 1790. One served as a Private in the Second Regiment of Sussex County Militia during the Revolution.

Sussex County – Hardiston Township
George Buchanan
Michael Buchanan
William Buchanan

All of these Buchanans are listed as Bohanon in the 1773-1774 tax list. As explained previously, many of these Bohanons either changed from this Scotch-Irish derivation of Buchanan back to the original clan name once they were in America or the census takers simply listed them under a name they knew.

Pennsylvania

Pennsylvania's history is not only parallel but intertwined with that of Delaware. The Dutch, Swedes and Finns all colonized areas around the Delaware River. The various nationality groups clashed over the land and eventually the British conquered the area in 1664. In 1681 William Penn arrived with Welsh settlers and Quakers. For a time after the Duke of York sold Delaware to Pennsylvania the two were treated as one colony, but in 1702 Delaware was politically separated from Pennsylvania.

Pennsylvania was established as a religiously- neutral zone among the colonies. Although the Quakers ruled the colony for a time, no formal religion was established in Pennsylvania even while other colonies adopted various denominations as state religions. Pennsylvania also became involved in the early days of the antislavery movement and in 1780 passed a law to gradually eliminate slavery by making the children of slaves free, culminating in complete abolition in 1847.

Compared to most colonies, the Indian wars affected the Pennsylvania settlers the hardest. As it moved westward, the frontier was a constant battleground between European settlers and Indians. The French and Indian War and then the Revolution were noted for the vicious Indian warfare along the frontier In each year frontier settlements and forts were attacked, many being destroyed, and many settlers were killed. Because of the frontier problems, and the inability of Quaker pacifism to ensure the safety of the settlers, the Quakers were replaced as the governing party of the colony.

Among those of Scottish lineage that moved to America, it was mainly the Scotch-Irish that came to Pennsylvania. Due to economic conditions in Ireland, large numbers arrived, especially in the early and mid-1700s. While the largest number sought out the western frontier and interior river valleys, some used Pennsylvania as a beginning point, moving further south to

24

Virginia and the Carolina frontiers. The counties in the Cumberland and Susquehanna River Valleys showed large numbers of Scotch-Irish among the early inhabitants.

Pennsylvania was not as large a magnet for those born in Scotland. As in other colonies, some Scots, especially merchants and indentured servants, settled in eastern cities. But no major Scottish immigration was found before 1790.

The 1790 population showed Pennsylvania to be one of the larger states, with 434,373 residents according to the Census Bureau. Among the large states, Pennsylvania had the fewest slaves with only 3,707 in 1790. It also had a growing population of free black residents, similar to New York City.

Pennsylvania Buchanans, 1790

There were many Buchanan families, mainly Scotch-Irish, who lived in Pennsylvania in 1790. The most notable in time was the family of James Buchanan whose parents had arrived in America from Ulster in 1783. However, Buchanan families had been arriving for a century before the census, many coming during the Scotch-Irish migration to America in the mid-1700s.

With the exception of some Buchanans in Chester County, and one in Philadelphia, most of the Buchanans were settled in areas away from the coast and the chief city. This was in line with the tendency of Scotch-Irish families to live away from the coast and on the frontier.

When it came to slavery in Pennsylvania, only the Buchanan families in Westmoreland and York Counties owned slaves, while Pennsylvania also had the most free black persons living with families with the name surname Buchanan. Three free blacks lived with Buchanan families in the state while only seven slaves were held by Buchanan families.

Allegheny County – Pitt Township
   Robert Buckhanen – one white male over 16, one female

Chester County – Fallowfield
   Eccles Buchannan – two white males over 16, four under 16, five females

   The son of John Buchanan, Eccles Buchanan, was born in 1762 in County Donegal, Ireland. He migrated to Pennsylvania in 1783, taking the oath of allegiance in 1785. He appears on tax rolls in West Fallowfield in1791-1793. Although the census lists him in Chester County, Pennsylvania in 1790, he was a shoemaker in Baltimore, Maryland in 1800 and in Hopewell Township, Washington County in 1810. He also appears in tax rolls for Hopewell Township beginning from 1805 to 1809. He married Ann (?) before 1786 and his eight children included Elizabeth, Margaret and Robert born before the 1790 census. He died in March 1814 and his will was proved that year in Washington County, Pennsylvania. Both he and Ann are buried in the Upper Buffalo Presbyterian Church Cemetery.

Chester County – Honey Brook
   Hannah Buchanan – two white males over 16, three under 16, four females

   Hannah Buchanan was the widow of a Buchanan she married in the 1770s. She may have been the widow of James Buchanan who died in 1788. His will contained a notation "Adm. to Hannah Buchanan". She was a member of the Presbyterian Church in the Forks of the Brandywine, 1792. Her will of 1804 lists John and Robert as executors. She died in 1805

   Matthew Buchanan – two white males over 16, two under 16, two females

   Matthew Buchanan married Martha (Boyer) (died 1820) and had children including sons John, Matthew and Samuel, and daughters Marget and Marthew. He was on the county tax rolls in 1780, 1785 and 1805. He was also a member of the Presbyterian Church in the Forks of the Brandywine. He died and his will was probated in 1807.

Samuel Buchanan – two white males over 16, six under 16, two females

Samuel Buchanan was listed in the 1786 Septennial Census of Pennsylvania. In 1796 he married Sarah (Piersol) and had a son Jesse. He appeared on the tax list of 1805 and in the wills of one of the Piersol family in 1813 and that of his mother-in-law in 1814, the same year that he died.

Chester County – Londonderry
David Buchanen – four white males over 16, five females

Allegedly born in Ireland, David Buchanen lived in Chester County from 1760 until his death. He was on the 1774 landowner list for the township. By trade he was a blacksmith prior to 1779. His family included his wife Margaret (Cochran) (Boggs), whom he married in January 1790 in Chester County and children Alexander, John, Jean/Jane, and Margaret. He was probably married previously with other children, a fact that might be reflected in the number of persons in the household when the census was taken. He died in 1798, with his will proved in 1799

Cumberland County - Hopewell Township
John Buchanan – two white males over 16, one under 16, three females

Robert Buchanon – one white male over 16, two females

Robert Buchanan, the son of Thomas Buchanan, served as a Private in the 8th Bn. of the Cumberland Co. Militia in 1782-1783. The next year he was a witness to a will in the township. Although he was single in 1790, he later married and had three children He was a member of the Big Spring Presbyterian Church. He died in Newville, Cumberland County in 1833.

Thomas Buchanan – four white males over 16, four under 16, seven females

Son of Robert Buchanan, Thomas Buchanan was born in County Tyrone, Ireland. During the Revolutionary War, he held several commands in the Pennsylvania Militia, including Captain of the 1st Pennsylvania Line. He fought at Boston, Long Island, White Plains, Trenton, Princeton, Brandywine, Paoli, Germantown and Monmouth. He was elected Sheriff of the county in 1789 and 1790. Thomas married a Miss (McFarlane) and had eight children. He was a member of the Big Spring Presbyterian Church. Thomas Buchanan died in 1823 in Newville, Cumberland County.

Waller Buchanan – three white males over 16, one under 16, one female

Waller Buchanan appears to also be the person listed in various places as Walker Buchanan and Walles Buchanan. He appears on the East Pennsborough tax list of 1750 under the name Walker Buchanan.

Walter Buchanan – three white males over 16, three under 16, one female

Son of William Buchanan, Walter Buchanan lived in East Pennsborough Township beginning in the 1760s. He witnessed numerous wills during the 1770s and 1780s and is mentioned in a 1776 deed description. He also served as an elder in his church in 1773.

The 1793 Septennial Census of Pennsylvania listed a number of persons who may have been part of the families listed here or may not have been in the 1790 census. The list includes a merchant named **Alexander Buchanan**, a farmer named **James Buchanan**, other **John Buchanans**, one **Robert Buchanan** listed as an Ensign, the other as a carpenter, and a carpenter named **William Buchanan**. There may be other Williams as well because one appears as a tailor in the 1805 tax list while another served in the Militia during the French and Indian War and kept a tavern in Carlisle in 1753. Another citation to William Buchanan was that he served as a Private in the Cumberland County Militia and was promoted Corporal in 1780. He married Catherine (?).

Alexander Buchanan

Alexander Buchanan was born in 1760 and died in 1810, the son of Thomas Buchanan of Cumberland County. He was a Captain in the Pennsylvania Line during the Revolution. He married Elizabeth (Leonard) (born 1772) in Cumberland County in 1796. In 1797 he moved to Meadville, Crawford County. His son Robert moved to Cincinnati, Ohio where he became a noted agriculturalist, businessman and civic leader. It is possible that in 1790 he was living with his father and did not appear in the U.S. census but did appear later in the Pennsylvania Septennial census.

James Buchanan

James Buchanan was born in 1749 in Cumberland County. He died in the county in 1829.

John Buchanan

John Buchanan was a tanner in East Caln Township, then owned a tannery near Wagontown, West Caln. He appears on many government documents including the East Pennsborough township tax lists of 1750 and 1762, the East Caln tax list of 1805, a deed in 1815 and wills of 1786, 1788 and 1814. He sold land in 1824. He served as a Captain of the 7th Bn. Cumberland County Militia in 1777. He married Dorcas (Galbreath) (born 1746, died 1810) and had children including James and Juliet. He was also guardian of a couple of other children.

John Buchanan

John Buchanan was born in 1755 in East Pennsborough Twp, Cumberland County. He was appointed as a tax collector in 1782. In 1786, John married Elizabeth (McCormick) (born 1761, died 1831) in Cumberland County. Of their six children, only Jane was born before the census.

John Buchanan

John Buchanan was born in 1757 in Cumberland County. He married Mary (?). He was listed as a farmer in Cumberland County in the 1783 Septennial census of Pennsylvania and he appeared on the 1782 tax collection list. Later the family moved to Poland Township, in Trumbull County, Ohio, where he was listed on the 1804 tax list.

Other information concerning John Buchanans in Cumberland County:

One John was a Private in the Cumberland County Militia.

One Buchanan owned one or more slaves according to the records of the Silver Spring Presbyterian Church, although the time frame is not stated beyond the last half of the 1700s.

Dauphin County
James Buchanon – five white males over 16, four under 16, five females

James Buchanan is noted in many documents regarding Dauphin County. In 1773 he was appointed as a county road supervisor. He was a resident of Upper Paxton Township in 1779. He received a land warrant in 1782 and another for 100 acres in 1786. He was listed in the 1786 Septennial Census of Pennsylvania as well as the 1790 federal census. He was on the list of property owners and both bought and sold land in the county during 1790. The same year he received a land grant in Georges Township. James Buchanan died in 1810 leaving wife Hannah and children Ann, Hannah, James, Jean, Joseph, Mary, Nathan, Nathaniel, Robert, Samuel, Sarah and William.

Fayette County
   Alexander Buchanan – three white males over 16, four under 16, four females

   Alexander Buchanan appears in the Pennsylvania's records in 1782 on an expedition against the Indians and in 1787 on the tax rolls of Fayette County. He bought land along Georges Creek in 1790.

George Buchanan

   It is believed that George Buchanan was born in Ireland in 1721, then migrated to York County, Pennsylvania in 1774. He served as a Private in the 4th Pennsylvania Line during the Revolution. He apparently moved to Kentucky about 1790 or 1791, appearing in the Woodford County, Kentucky tax rolls from 1792-1795. There is confusion about this family line with several conflicting genealogies.

   There is another possible **George Buchanan** in Fayette County in 1790. Born in County Donegal, Ireland in 1769, this George Buchanan married Rebecca (?) in 1789 in Fayette County. He died in the county in 1828.

Franklin County
   Christy Buchanon – one white male over 16, two under 16, four females

   Thomas Buchanon – three white males over 16, three under 16, three females

   Thomas Buchanon was a 3rd Lieutenant in the Revolutionary War.

31

Franklin County – Fannet, Hamilton, Letterkenny, Montgomery and Peters
        George Buchanon – two white males over 16, two females
        George Buchanan – one white male over 16, two females

        One of the George Buchanans is listed as George Buckhannon in the county's 1786 tax list.

        James Buchanon – one white male over 16, one under 16, one female

        James Buchanan – one white male over 16, two females

        Born in Ramelton, County Donegal, Ireland in the 1760s, this future father of the President came to Pennsylvania in 1783 and lived at Cove Gap near Harrisburg. In 1788, James married Elizabeth (Speer) (born 1767, Lancaster County, Pennsylvania, died 1783, Greensburg, Pennsylvania). At the time of the 1790 census the couple had only one child named Mary, but ten others would come later, including the future President in 1791. James Buchanan was appointed auditor of an estate in 1809. This James Buchanan died in 1821 in Mercersburg.

        One of the two men named James Buchanan was county auditor in 1800-1802.

        John Buchanon – one white male over 16, three under 16, two females

        Listed as John Buckhannon in the 1786 tax list, this man also received a land warrant in 1787 for his service in the Cumberland County Militia during the Revolution. He received his service pension in 1818.
.

Also found in Franklin County, but not on the census, is **Alexander Buchanan** who was born in 1756, who lived near Mercersburg and had children in 1770 and 1774. He served as a Private in the Pennsylvania Line in the Revolution then returned home to Mercersburg until his death in 1819.

Huntingdon County
George Bucannon – two white males over 16

George Buchanan settled in Huntingdon County in 1775 or 1785 (depending on the source) then appeared on the list of Huntingdon County men eligible to be in the Militia in 1788. He died in the county in 1802.

Marey Bucannon – one white male under 16, two females

Lancaster County – Drumore
James Buchannon – four white males over 16, one under 16, four females

Son of Thomas and Rachel (Williamson) Buchanan, James Buchannon hired a substitute for his service in the Revolutionary War. He married Agnes (Turner) in Lancaster in 1771. Listed as a road contractor in 1796, his will was made in 1798. He is mentioned in the county history books.

According to a local history[2], there was a **John Buchanan**, Esquire who lived in the township from 1755 to the early 1800s.

Lancaster County - Little Britain –
Gilbert Buchannon – three white males over 16, two under 16, five females

Son of Walter and Jean (McLaughlin) Buchanan, Gilbert Buchanan was born in Chester County in 1750. In 1773 he married Sarah (Walker) and obtained land in Lancaster County the same year. He was mentioned in his father's will, which was proved in 1787. By 1790 the family had children including Isaac, Mary, Rebecca, Sarah and Walter. In 1803 the family moved to Poland Township in Ohio, where he appeared in the 1804 tax list.

James Buchannon – two white males over 16, two females

The son of Walter and Jean (McLaughlin) Buchanan, this James Buchanan was born in Little Britain, Lancaster County in 1761. He served in Morrison's Battalion of the Pennsylvania Militia during the Revolutionary War. He was listed in his father's will of 1787. He married Margaret (Ross) and lived in Hanover Township. Of their ten children at least one, Elizabeth, was born prior to 1790.

Widow Buchannon – one white male over 16, one under 16, four females

The widow mentioned in the census was probably Jean (McLaughlin) Buchanan, the widow of Walter who died in 1787. She was mentioned in his will and both Gilbert and James lived in the area.

Luzerne County
William Buchanan – three white males over 16; one under 16, three females

Mifflin County
Arthur Buchanan – one white male over 16, one under 16, one female

Arthur Buchanan – one white male over 16, two under 16, four females, one free black person

One of these Arthur Buchanans was a merchant.

Another **Arthur Buchanan** was born in 1740, the son of Arthur and Dorcas (Holt) Buchanan. Known as Arthur, Jr., he served as a Colonel in the Revolutionary War. On the county tax lists in 1773, and 1782 he married Margery (?). He also apparently served as a juror for the first county court of common pleas in 1789. Arthur died in 1811 without issue according to the Pioneers of Mifflin County[3].

Joseph Buchanan – one white male over 16, one under 16, four females

Robert Buchanan – one white male over 16, four under 16, four females

Robert Buchanan, another son of Arthur and Dorcas (Holt) Buchanan, was born in 1749 and died in 1849. He married Lucinda (Landrum) and operated a trading post in Maryland. He and Lucinda had ten children, with those born prior to 1790 including Andrew, Arthur, Dorcas, Jane, Mary, Rebecca and William.

Northumberland County
James Buchanan – three white males over 16, two females

James Buchanan was mentioned as in a court case in 1773, then as one of the inhabitants of White Deer in 1778. He served as a Private in the Northumberland County Militia during the Revolution and remained on the 1782 muster rolls. He is also mentioned in a property description for land in a neighbor's estate in 1788.

Bell's History of Northumberland County[4] lists a **John Buchanan** in the 1780s. He was apparently a surveyor who is mentioned in two surveys of land warrants in 1782 as well as a letter about surveying that year. He was a member of the Warrior Run Presbyterian Church in 1789.

Philadelphia – Northern Liberties Township
John Buchannon – one white male over 16, four under 16, two females

A 1782 letter addressing surveyors named John Buchanan includes the reference to Northern Liberties Township. This may be the same John Buchanan as mentioned in the Northumberland County history.

Washington County
Elizabeth Buchannon/Buckhannan – one white male over 16, four under 16, four females

James Bucchannon – single white male
James Buchannon – one white male over 16, four under 16, three females
James Buchannon - two white males over 16, two under 16, seven females

With so many people of the same name, it is hard to determine which James Buchanan is which. Two of the James Buchanans were listed on the Septennial Census of Pennsylvania in 1786. One served as a Captain in the Revolution and owned land in South Strabane Township in 1780. He may have been the same one who served in William's expedition against the Indians. At least one was mentioned as a witness to wills between 1789 and 1791.

Walter Buchannon – one white male over 16, one female

Walter Buchanan was born in 1760 and died in 1807 in the county, his will being proved in 1807. He married Elizabeth (Clarke) (born 1764, died 1838) and received land in the county in 1787 and 1788. He was an executor of an estate in 1799.

William Buchannon – two white males over 16, two under 16, four females

William Buchannon, born in Ireland in 1738, served in Cpt. Scott's Co. of the Washington County Militia during the Revolutionary War. He was married but his wife died in 1791. He died in 1814 in Washington County but his daughter moved to Ohio.

Washington County – Armstrong
Cristefor Buchannon – single white male

Christopher Buchanan married Mary (?) and lived in Washington County until 1801 when he sold his land. This may be the Christopher Buchanan who was born in County Donegal, Ireland in 1764 and died in German Township, Fayette County in 1851. If it is the same, he became a naturalized citizen and married Mary Ann (Robinson) in 1798 in Washington County and had at least eight and as many as 12 children.

Hanover Township
John Buchannon – one white male over 16, three under16, three females

John Buchannon served in the Revolutionary War. He lived in Hanover Township and was listed as a merchant in 1800. He was listed as a farmer and blacksmith on a 1799 bond.

Hopewell Township
Jno/John Buchannon/Buckhannan –three white males over 16, four under 16, three females

John Buchanan was born in County Tyrone, Ireland in 1730 and died around 1795 in Washington County. In 1766 he married Mary (Jean) (Ross) in Philadelphia. John served in the French and Indian War, fighting at Fort Pitt. He then served in Cpt. Miller's Company of Washington County Militia in 1782. He was a resident of Hopewell Township listed in the 1786 Septennial

Census of Pennsylvania. Some of his children moved to Ohio and others to the part of Virginia that later became West Virginia.

Boyd Crumrine's county history[5] lists a **Samuel Buchanan** in Hopewell Township. Born in 1743 in Lancaster County, Samuel Buchanan moved to Hopewell Township, Washington County in 1783. He is listed as a landowner in 1785. He married Elizabeth (Adams) and had 11 children. Samuel Buchanan died in 1794. Samuel is buried at the Lower Buffalo Cemetery.

In addition, **George Buchanan**, lived in Washington County, Pennsylvania. Born in 1767, he married in 1790 and lived in Washington County until his death in 1843. There is also mentioned a **John Buchanan** who signed a petition in Cross Creek Township in 1789 and another who signed a petition of residents of Donegal Township in 1793.

Westmoreland County
David Buckhanon – two white males over 16, two under 16, three females

Westmoreland County – Fairfield
John Buckhanan – one white male over 16, six under 16, three females, five slaves

Born about 1725 in Ireland, he settled in York County before the Revolutionary War. He was a Ranger in the Pennsylvania Militia during the Revolutionary War and a 1st Lt. of the 6th Bn., York County Militia. He married twice, the second being Jane (Rowan) (born 1740, Lancaster County, died 1814). He was one of only two Buchanans families in Pennsylvania to hold slaves in 1790. He died in Chanceford Township, York County in 1810, leaving several children. There is confusion about Ms. Rowan's name as the marriage record lists her name as Jean, John's pension application lists her as Jane, and the cemetery record lists her as Jean.

York County

Robert Buchannon – one white male over 16, three under 16, five females

Robert Buchanan served in the 2nd Co., 5th Bn. of Washington County Militia in 1778. He was listed as an attorney in the county in 1783 and appears in the 1786 Septennial Census of Pennsylvania.

Walter Buchannon – one white male over 16, four females

Walter Buchanan was listed in the 1786 Septennial Census of Pennsylvania.

William Buchanan – three white males over 16, one under 16, three females

This William Buchanan moved to Hamilton County, Ohio in the late 1790s and owned land in Warren County, Ohio. He died in 1799 leaving a wife and eight children.

York County – Chanceford

William Buchanan – one white male over 16, one under 16, one female

William Buckanan – one white male over 16, one female

One of the William Buchanans was born about 1761, the son of John Buchanan. One was a member of the United Presbyterian Church of Chanceford.

York County – Cumberland Township

Andrew Buchanan – three white males over 16, four under 16, six females

Born in 1766, the son of John Buchanan, Andrew Buchanan and his family lived in Cumberland Township in the

1790s according to tax records. He also witnessed a deed in 1784. The area in which they lived would become part of Adams County at the creation of that county in 1800. Among the children were daughters Catherine and Elizabeth.

York County – Fawn Township
    Patt Buchanan – single white male

    Samuel Buchanan – one white male over 16, one under 16, one female, one free black person

    Samuel Buchanan owned 310 acres in 1783 but sold some of his land in 1789.

York County – Hopewell Township
    William Buchanan – single white male over 16

York County – Monaghan Township
    Widow Buckhanan – one white male over 16, four females

York County – Mount Pleasant
    Henry Buchannon – one white male over 16, two under 16, three females, a free black person, two slaves

    Born about 1761, Henry Buchannon and his wife lived in Gettysburg in Mount Pleasant beginning in 1779. That year he served as a Private in Andrew's Co., 10th Bn. Washington County Militia. He appears on tax records throughout the 1780s. The interesting fact is that there was both a free black person and two slaves in the household. Often a free black would own slaves as a way to free family members who were held as slaves. There is no indication one way or the other as to whether this was the situation in this household. Henry did sign a verification that a free black man served in the Revolutionary War with him. This verification may have been for the same man who lived with the family in 1790.

There also appears to have been an **Andrew Buchanan** in Newberry Township. He signed a petition to the Legislature in 1756 and appears in the tax records of the 1790s before his death in 1794. He married Elizabeth (?) and had a daughter Elizabeth, both named in his will.

Delaware

An independent state by 1790, during its colonial period Delaware was originally part of Virginia, then New York, then Pennsylvania. Governor De La Warr (hence the name of the state) claimed the land in the current state as part of Virginia's claim to all the lands around the Chesapeake Bay. This claim was short-lived as other nations would colonize it and it would not return to British dominance until 1664 when it was regained as the British drove out the Dutch who claimed it as part of their territory.

Once the Dutch East India Company became interested in commercial pursuits in the New World, several Dutch settlements were planted in modern Delaware between 1624 and 1631. They were driven out by Indians but returned again and in 1651 began what is now New Castle. In the meantime, the Swedish interest in the land led to a 1638 settlement in what is now part of Wilmington. Joined by Finns, the immigrants of both nations settled in modern Pennsylvania and Delaware on both sides of the Delaware River.

The Dutch drove out the Swedes and Finns in 1655, but in 1664 the British conquered the territory and ended Dutch control. At that point the Governor of New York claimed New Jersey and Delaware as part of the northern colony. This claim lasted until 1682 when the Duke of York sold his rights in the area to William Penn who arrived that year with charters for both Pennsylvania the Lower Colonies on the Delaware.

After 1704, the governance of Delaware was overseen by Pennsylvania but not under its control and influence. In 1702 a Charter of Privileges was established including a separate legislature for Delaware. This legislature enacted separate laws, although a common governorship existed until the Revolution. Its three counties became an independent state in 1776 and later it became the first state to ratify the Constitution of the United States.

Although the census records of Delaware were among those either burned by the British or lost, the Census Bureau lists the 1790 population at 59,094. Being a slaveholding state, Delaware had 8,887 slaves in 1790.

The Scottish population was never large in Delaware compared to other states. As a result, the reconstructed census for the states only lists two Buchanans, although others appear to have been living in the state in 1790. The two listed families are

New Castle County – Appoquinimink Hundred
James Buchanan

James Buchanan was a single man who died prior to 1816.

Sussex County – Northwest Fork Hundred
Sarah Buchanan, widow

From marriage records, it appears that Sarah Buchanan married Jesse Green in 1790 and died shortly thereafter.

Although not listed in the reconstructed census, a **James Buchanan** lived in Sussex County during this period. He owned a home and land in Broad Creek Hundred, Sussex County as seen in land records of 1789, 1793 and 1807. He is also mentioned in the "Sussex County Orphan Court Extracts, 1770-1830."

It is possible that a third Buchanan was present in Delaware at the time of the census. A **Mary Buchanan** of

Middleton, New Castle County, is listed in the Delaware Grave Index as dying in 1790. Born in 1744, she was 46 years old at the time of death. Because the census was taken in August, 1790, if she died after that date, she should have appeared in the census; otherwise, she would not have been counted.

Further apart in time is **David Buckhanin** who was a Private from Delaware in the Revolutionary War. There is no indication that he still lived in New Jersey in 1790, but due to the problem of reconstructing the census, he may still have been in the state at that time.

---

[1] Kenn Stryker-Rodda. *Revolutionary Census of New Jersey: An Index, Based on Rateables, of the Inhabitants of New Jersey During the Period of the American Revolution* (Lambertville, New Jersey: Hunterdon House, 1986).

[2] Aaron S. Ely, *The Long Family of Drumore Township, Lancaster County, Pennsylvania.* (1909).

[3] John Stroup and Raymond Bell. *Pioneers of Mifflin County.* (Lewistown, Pennsylvania, 1942).

[4] Herbert C. Bell, *History of Northumberland County, Pennsylvania* (Chicago: Brown, Runk & Co., Publishers, 1891).

[5] Boyd Crumrine, *History of Washington County, Pennsylvania with Biographical Sketches of Many of Its Pioneers and Prominent Men* (Philadelphia: L. H. Leverts & Co., 1882).

Chapter Three

UPPER SOUTH

The Upper South was the first region of the country to develop its potential. As a result, by 1790, Virginia far outstripped the rest of the nation in population and wealth. New York, by contrast, was fifth in population at that time. This may have been due to the early settlement of Virginia in 1607 or due to a lack of serious disputes to the colony's English rule. Obviously tobacco played an important role as America's first cash crop for European markets. Maryland's addition to the region was the fact that it was the only Catholic-based colony which allowed certain European groups to migrate without fear of persecution. By 1790 the combined population of the two states was more than one million.

People of Scottish heritage were deeply involved in both of the Upper South colonies, later states. As with many other areas, Scottish immigrants settled in the Eastern part of the colony, while Scotch-Irish moved to the river valleys and frontiers. Scottish tobacco traders, factors and merchants established mercantile businesses in the Virginia ports and Scottish Catholics migrated to Maryland. Scots and Scotch-Irish settlers also created large farms on the Eastern Shore of Maryland and Virginia in the 1600s. The Scotch-Irish often moved south from Pennsylvania into Virginia and down the Shenandoah Valley then into Kentucky and Tennessee.

The Upper South was also the heart of slavery in America in 1790. Virginia and Maryland accounted for 57% of the slaves in the United States in 1790. Many of the businesses and plantations of the East relied on slave labor. The Buchanans of these states followed the general pattern and the great majority of them in the two states owned slaves as well.

Maryland

Maryland was settled in 1633 as the first Catholic colony in the modern United States. Due to conflict with Protestants who also came to Maryland, the Tolerance Act was passed in 1649 making Maryland a colony that would tolerate people of any Christian religion. But the clash between religious groups continued as Puritan groups moved into the northern part of the colony, establishing Annapolis in 1650, and revolting against the colonial rulers until 1658. Maryland also faced land and border disputes over land claimed by both Pennsylvania and Maryland. These disputes led to Cresap's War which involved the mobilization of the Maryland Militia in 1736 and the Pennsylvania Militia in 1737. King George III compelled a cease fire and peace agreement between the two colonies in 1738.

Maryland's land dispute with Pennsylvania ended with the adoption in 1767 of the survey of the boundary by Charles Mason and Jeremiah Dixon. Unlike Pennsylvania and Virginia, Maryland had fewer military problems during the Indian wars. Similarly, no major battles were fought in the colony during the Revolutionary War.

While the Scottish Catholics settled the Baltimore area in the 1630s and 1640s, Scotch-Irish settlers originally moved into the Eastern Shore in the 1600s. The Baltimore merchant class had many Scottish individuals, while many other Scots were present in the area solely due to their religion and their escape from the religious wars of Europe.

By 1790, the population of Maryland was 319,728 according to the Census Bureau. There were 103,026 slaves in the colony, third among the colonies after Virginia and South Carolina.

Buchanans in 1790 Maryland

The Buchanan families of Maryland were scattered throughout the state except for the far west. These families were areas around Baltimore and as far west as Frederick. No settled in several of the Eastern Shore counties, along with the Buchanans were found in the three western counties on the frontier.

Most of the Buchanan families owned slaves. In Baltimore, these may have been household slaves or worked in the city's businesses, but in the rural areas, they worked farms and plantations. The most slaves were owned by a Susannah Buchanan, a resident of Black River Upper Hundred in Baltimore County, who owned 20 slaves. Others in Baltimore City and the "hundreds" of Baltimore County owned 22 slaves. Numbers were generally not as high in the outlying areas, although one person owned 11 slaves in Montgomery County and another owned 9 slaves in Kent County.

Baltimore City
Andrew Buchanan – two white males over 16, two under 16, two slaves

The 1783 tax list shows that Andrew owned eight parcels of land in Back River Upper Hundred and Middle River Upper Hundred, Baltimore County.

George Buchanan – two white males over 16, one under 16, two females, three slaves

Among the most famous of the early Buchanan was Dr. George Buchanan, son of Andrew and Susan (Lawson) Buchanan. Born in 1763, George Buchanan was educated in Philadelphia, then at the University of Edinburgh in Scotland and the University of Paris. While overseas, he was President of the Royal Physician's Society of Edinborough. He returned to the United States in 1788, and married Letetia (McKean) the next year.

Together they had 11 children. As a doctor, George Buchanan established a hospital in Baltimore, served on the Baltimore City Council in 1797, then took a job in Philadelphia where he died in 1808. Ironically, while he was an early abolitionist, George owned three slaves.

James Buchanan – three white males over 16, five females, one slave

One of two James Buchanans at the time of the census, this was James A. Buchanan, Baltimore merchant and son of George and Eleanor (Rogers) Buchanan. Born in 1744, James married Elizabeth (?) and had seven children.

William Buchanan – 2 white males over 16, 1 under 16, 5 females, 4 slaves

The son of George and Eleanor (Rogers) Buchanan, William Buchanan was born in 1748 in Baltimore. He was a member of the Maryland Provincial Council in 1774-1775, the Committee of Correspondence in 1775 and 1776, and he served in the Baltimore Militia in 1776. He became a General of Maryland forces during the Revolutionary War and served as the Commissary-General of the American forces in 1777-1778. Appointed as the Baltimore County of Wills in 1778, he served until his death in 1834. He owned land in the Delaware Upper Hundred according to the 1783 tax list. He first married Margaret (Dorsey) (born 1752, Anne Arundel County, died 1797) in 1772 and had 12 children. Following Margaret's death, he married Hephzibah (Brown) and had either two or four more children (depending on source). He received two slaves from his father's estate and had a runaway slave, Henry, listed in the February 1, 1778 Baltimore Advertiser. He was also a member of the Westminster Presbyterian Church of Baltimore. He died in 1824.

There were other Buchanans in 1790 Baltimore, including **Alexander Pitt Buchanan, Archibald Buchanan** and **Robert Buchanan**. There was also a second **George Buchanan, James**

Buchanan and **William Buchanan** in Baltimore at the time of the census.

Alexander Pitt Buchanan was born in Baltimore in 1765, the son of Andrew and Susan (Lawson) Buchanan. He married Sarah (Hite) (born 1775) in 1794. Alexander died in Frederick County, Virginia and his children moved to Tennessee.

The son of Andrew and Susan(nah) (Lawson) Buchanan, **Andrew Buchanan** was born in Baltimore in 1766. He was single at the time of the census. In 1797 he married first, Ann (McKean) (born 1773, New Castle, Delaware; died 1804, Baltimore) in Philadelphia and they had three children after 1790. After Ann's death, he married Caroline Virginia Mary (Johnson) in Boston in 1807. They had a son , Robert Christie Buchanan. Andrew died in 1811.

Archibald Buchanan was born in Baltimore in 1737, the son of George and Eleanor (Rogers) Buchanan. He is noted on a lease of Baltimore commercial property in 1763. After serving on the Committee of Correspondence, he was appointed tax commissioner of Baltimore County in 1777. In 1783 he was living in Baltimore but was also listed as a property owner on the Back River, Upper Hundred and Middle River Upper Hundred land assessments. He married Sarah (Lee) in 1800 in Baltimore. Archibald Buchanan died in Baltimore in 1800.

George Buchanan is listed in the 1783 tax assessment as owning land in both the city of Baltimore and the county. Because the physician George Buchanan was out of the country being educated at the time, there may have been another George Buchanan in the county. Otherwise, it is possible that George Buchanan already had land from his parents prior to going abroad for his education.

Born in 1768, **James Buchanan** married Ann (?). He died in 1840.

References to a second **William Buchanan** can be found in the book <u>Baltimore: Past and Present</u>[1]. During the Revolution Lt. William Buchanan wrote a letter to Brigadier General William Buchanan. A Cpt. William Buchanan was tried in 1791 for murder arising from a duel involving a David Sterrett. No punishment occurred because Cpt. Buchanan was fighting Indians as part of the St. Clair expedition in the Northwest Territories and was wounded during a 1792 battle there.

Baltimore County - Back River – Upper Hundred
   Susannah Buchannan – one white male over 16, seven females, twenty slaves.

   Susannah Buchanan was listed as a widow who died in 1798.

Baltimore County – East Hundred
   Ellianor Buchanan

   Ellianor Buchanan was on the 1783 tax lists with property in several of the "Hundreds" of Baltimore County.

   Matthew Buchanan

   Matthew Buchanan is listed in the 1783 tax assessments as owning land in East Hundred.

Baltimore County – Gunpowder Upper Hundred
   Cpt. Buchanan

   Captain Buchanan is on the 1783 tax assessment list for the county. This could be the same person as found in Montgomery County in 1790. He may also have owned land in Baltimore County in 1783.

Baltimore County – Middlesex Hundred
Samuel Buchanan

Samuel Buchanan is listed on the 1783 tax assessment list for the county.

Baltimore County - Patapsco – Lower Hundred
Arter Buckhanan – two white males over 16, two females

Arthur Buchanan is listed in the 1783 land assessment.

An entry listed as **"negroes of William Buchaneneus"**– 8 slaves

William Buchanan is not listed here. These are probably the slaves of William Buchanan of Baltimore who owned land in the county as well as the city.

Cecil County - Back Creek
Margaret Buchanan – two white males over 16, five females, two slaves

Cecil County – North Milford
James Buchanan – two white males over 16, three under 16, one female, one slave

James Buchanan was an overseer of roads in Cecil County in 1760.

John Buchanan – two white males over 16, two under 16, four females

Frederick
Dr. John Buchanan – two white males over 16, four under 16, one female, one slave

Dr. John Buchanan appears on the 1783 land assessment rolls and signed a road petition in March 1788. He also had a claim against a 1792 estate and was a trustee in an insolvency proceeding in 1805. He had a daughter Polly.

William Buchanan – single white male over 16

Kent County – James Buchanan – single white male over 16, nine slaves

James Buchanan was a member of the Maryland legislature, 1765-1768. He signed a road petition for the county in 1766.

Robert Buchanan – family data illegible

Robert Buchanan owned several pieces of land shown on the 1783 land assessment rolls. He was appointed to the Maryland House of Delegates as a representative from Kent County.

Montgomery County
Cpt. Buchannen – eleven (?) white males over 16

Queen Anne's County
Nathaniel Buchanan – three white males over 16, four under 16, three females, two slaves

Nathaniel Buchanan witnessed a deed in 1774.

St. Mary's County

There were no Buchanans listed in the 1790 census for St. Mary's County. Regardless, there are two Buchanan families which appear in numerous county records of that period.

George Buchanan, Jr., the son of George and Eleanor (Rogers) Buchanan was born in Maryland in 1738 and died in

1797 in St. Mary's County. He served as a Private in the Maryland Militia in the Revolution. He was appointed tax commissioner of St. Mary's County in 1777. George married Elizabeth (Holland) (died 1798, St. Mary's County) and had 12 children, all born before 1790. These were Catherine, Edward, Elizabeth, Fidelia, George, Henry, James, Jesse, Jonathan, Joseph, Rebecca and Richard.

One of those recorded in St. Mary's County was **Jonathan Buchanan** who was born in 1767 and died in 1838 in St. Mary's County. He was the son of George and Elizabeth (Holland) Buchanan and may have been living with his parents in 1790. He married Mary (Richardson) (born 1777, St. Mary's County) in 1796 and had two children. Jonathan changed his family name to Bohanan.

Worcester County
    John Buchanan – one white male over 16, four under 16, five females, eleven slaves

John Buchanan is listed on the 1788 tax list. He died in July 1834.

Virginia

The earliest permanent English settlement in America was in Virginia, and the first commercial crop for the colonies was developed there. After the Jamestown settlement of 1607, small settlements grew in the early 1600s, but the discovery of tobacco as a cash crop began the era of larger plantations and farms as well as commercial trade to Europe. Of all the colonies, Virginia became the most "English" in character.

Although Virginia began as a commercial enterprise, it became a crown colony in 1642. With the 1693 establishment of William & Mary College as America's second college after

Harvard, the commercial colony also became an educational center. With growing agriculture and trade, it is no surprise that by 1790, Virginia was the largest state in population with nearly 25% of the country's people. Not only was it the state with the largest population, but it also had far more slaves than any other state with 292.627 slaves.

Virginia took an early interest in dealing with the Indians on the frontier and exploring the area beyond the Appalachian Mountains. Traders and surveyors traveled the Ohio River Valley and the lands of modern West Virginia and Kentucky. Not only was the intention to protect Virginia's frontier, but also to solidify its claim to regions beyond the mountains. In this role, George Washington and three companions crossed the Blue Ridge

Mountains to survey in 1748, then was involved in surveying much of the western part of the Virginia Colony. After the French and Indian wars ended, Washington and another crew surveyed the lands on the Eastern bank of the Ohio River in modern West Virginia.

Both the French and Indian War and the Revolution heavily involved Virginia. Washington's role in both wars is part of history, but his knowledge of the land on the frontier came from his time as a surveyor. As a soldier, Washington had been in the militia since age 19, then rose through the ranks working alongside the British in the war against the French. As the leader of the colonial forces in the Revolution, both Washington and Virginia could not avoid the war and the ultimate end of the major combat in the Revolutionary War occurred at Williamsburg in 1781.

Scottish settlers came to Virginia early with an interest in the tobacco trade. As with so many of the colonies, Scots tended to collect on the East coast and centered around business interests, whether plantations or traders. Many of the Scots in Virginia were loyalists during the Revolution, and many left the state after independence was achieved. Virginia Scots generally moved to Canada as United Empire Loyalists.

The Scotch-Irish, on the other hand, were opposed to Britain as their ancestors had opposed England in the wars in Scotland. This group settled in the Shenandoah Valley and along the Blue Ridge Mountains. By 1790, some of them had crossed into the counties along the Ohio River. Many had fought in Ohio and would eventually cross the river to populate the new state. By 1790 the population of the western counties was 55,873 compared to 691,737 in the remainder of the state. There were fewer slaves in the western counties, partly because they were not the center of the larger plantations and commercial farms.

The census records for 1790 Virginia have been lost or were burned. As a result, the reconstructed census is only as close as one can provide for the state. Most of the Buchanans which would have appeared in the census are described in Lyman Chalkey's work on Southwest Virginia.[2] A few additional Buchanans may be found in tax records compiled by Augusta B. Fothergill and John M. Naugle.[3] Because these records reflect a period prior to 1790, there is some variation in the 1790 population, which can create some confusion.

Buchanans in 1790 Virginia

The Buchanan families listed in Fothergill are those close in time to the 1790 census. However, as in other areas, there are others that were not listed even in the Reconstructed Census. Local histories, church, tax and probate records also list a few Buchanan family members in Virginia not found in Fothergill.

One real problem found in searching for Buchanans in Virginia is that in certain counties there were numbers of people with the same name. In Southwestern Virginia in particular there may be references to a name but one has to try and match that record to a particular Buchanan. For Augusta, Washington, Wythe and somewhat in Rockbridge County, there are multiples of almost every given name Buchanan.

The classic example is the name John Buchanan. There are at least five John Buchanans with families in these areas, and some of those families have intermarrying Buchanans. One finds references to a Colonel John Buchanan, two Captain John Buchanans, a Yeoman John Buchanan, a John Buchanan of Beverly Manor and just plain John Buchanan. Sometimes there are mistaken references to a Major John Buchanan who moved to Tennessee, but he was not a Virginia resident prior to that move and only one of his family lived in Washington County, Virginia. A similar problem exists with James Buchanans in those counties. What is worse is that similar genealogies found in the various genealogical sources have names, dates and locations which differ for the same person. A birth date that has a range of 20 years, or birth location in either the United States or Ireland, or the names of children and spouses can be confused by those creating their genealogies. In some cases, the genealogies were created during the Buchanan scam of the 1930s, especially in cases where the original person came from Pennsylvania.

For reference purposes, one can start with Captain John Buchanan, who married Margaret (Campbell). They lived in Chester County, Pennsylvania and moved to Augusta County. He was apparently married once prior to his marriage to Margaret as he had six or seven children prior to their marriage. The couple then had six more children all born in Augusta County.

Two of the children of John and Margaret (Campbell) are of note. The first was Colonel John Buchanan who married Margaret (Patton) and arrived in Augusta County in 1741. Their son John was killed in the Revolutionary War but their son James lived in Rockbridge County and raised a family there.

The second child of John and Margaret (Campbell) Buchanan of note was Martha, born in 1738 or 1739. She married a Captain John Buchanan, son of James and Martha (Allison). John was born in Chester County, Pennsylvania but his family moved to Augusta County a decade later. Many of their children ended up in Wythe County while John and Martha moved to what later became Smyth County. His siblings, the children of James and Martha (Allison) Buchanan's and the family that moved with them from Chester County, Pennsylvania were found in Wythe County in 1790.

All this is to show that references to various Buchanan names, especially that of John or James Buchanan, is often confusing. As a result, unless it is known for certain, the list that follows will not identify all of the children of each family. Similarly, references in tax records and deeds may be all that identifies a person from the Fothergill list even though they might have a connection to one of these families. Also, even though the author has tried to match these documents and names, each person who is researching their ancestors should check the original sources to make certain they are correctly assigned.

With all of this in mind, the following are the Virginia Buchanans recorded from the various sources.

Augusta County
Alexander Buchanan – family of four

Alexander listed his wife Jean in his 1791 will. He had two children in 1790. The same year he was listed on the personal property tax list. He was appointed as a county tax commissioner in 1793. It is uncertain when or if the will was probated.

Andrew Buchanan

Andrew Buchanan witnessed a number of official records including probate records in the 1780s and two deeds in February and March 1790. He is also listed as A. Buchanan in some documents.

David Buchanan – white male and wife Sarah

Son of James and Mary (Reside) Buchanan, David Buchanan was born in 1749 in Augusta County. His brother George deeded his land to David in 1782. In 1781, David Buchanan became a Lieutenant in the Virginia military and was promoted to Captain in 1794 as he continued to serve through 1796 in the Augusta County Militia. He appeared on the 1790 personal property tax list. In 1797, David Buchanan became an attorney in Augusta County. He may have married Sarah (Caldwell) on April 13, 1789. He did marry Susanna (Ware) and had several children. Susanna and the children are mentioned in David's will of 1815. His children include Betsey, George, Hugh, James, Peggy and Polly. Susanna and the children are mentioned in his 1815 will. David Buchanan died in Augusta County in 1818.

James Buchanan

James Buchanan was a merchant in the 1760s and on the personal property tax list of 1790. He created a power of attorney in 1787. Court records list him as a Defendant in lawsuits in 1790 and 1791.

John Buchanan

Rambling Roots lists this John Buchanan as being born in Ireland in 1714 and passing away in Augusta County in 1790. This appears to be the person who is referred to as Captain John Buchanan who was probably actually born about 1700. The various sources list a birth date of 1700 to 1714 in County Tyrone, Ireland. However, since he had children beginning with Colonel John Buchanan in 1720, he could not have been born in 1714. He was apparently a miller by trade. He married Margaret (Campbell) (born about 1738, Ireland, died 1800, Augusta County) in 1738 and had six children with him. John already had seven children born from, 1720 to early 1730s, when he married Margaret. He died in 1790 in Augusta County.

Mary Buchanan – single white female

According to the will of James Buchanan, who died in 1761, his wife Mary was to receive his property provided she did not remarry. Although there is no positive identification of this Mary Buchanan, it appears this could be the widow of James Buchanan. She is listed as a witness to a deed in 1791.

Patrick Buchanan – 2 white males over age 16

The son of John and Margaret Buchanan, Patrick Buchanan was born in 1741 in Chester County, Pennsylvania shortly before the family moved to Augusta County. He was appointed as a surveyor in 1773, then served as a Captain in the Revolutionary War, fighting at the Battle of Cowpens. He witnessed a will in 1784 and appeared in the 1790 personal property tax list. Patrick married America (Copenhaver) and moved from Virginia in 1792, dying in Georgia about 1799.

Robert Buchanan

Robert Buchanan and his wife Martha witnessed a deed in 1789, bought land in 1793 and then sold land in 1779 and 1794.

Samuel Buchanan – wife Rebecca

Samuel married Rebecca (Sawyers) on December 30, 1790. They were involved in a lawsuit over land in 1796.

William Buchanan

William Buchanan was a surveyor by profession. He served as an Ensign in Cpt. McCutcheon's Co. during the Revolutionary War. He was listed as Buckhannon on the 1790 personal property tax list. He also served as an executor on an estate in 1791, the same year that he died.

Others that are listed in Augusta County about 1790 include a second **David Buchanan**, a **John Buchanan, Jr.**, **Richard Buchanan**, and two other **William Buchanans**

There is a second **David Buchanan** listed in the county records. The son of one of the John Buchanans, he was born in the 1760s. His will of December 1821 mentions his wife Sarah and children Jane and Mary. The will was probated in 1822.

John Buchanan, Jr. was born in Washington County in 1761. He married Nancy (Wright) and had ten children, all after 1790. He died in the county in 1831.

Richard Buchanan was a collector of revenue in Augusta County in 1785. He was also listed as a Defendant in a lawsuit that year.

One **William Buchanan** was an attorney in the county in the 1790s and 1800s. Another **William Buchanan** married Isabella (?) and had children Alexander, James and John before his death in 1805.

Bedford County
Theodore Buchanan

Son of Henry and Sarah (Armistead) Buchanan, Theodore Buchanan was born in 1758 in Bedford County, and married Elizabeth (Nimmo) there on January 17, 1789. He was also on the 1789 personal property tax list as Buckhannon. His second marriage was to Elizabeth (Huntsman) in Botetourt County in 1800. He had at least five children. David Buchanan died in Botetourt County sometime after the 1820 census.

There was also a **Sarah Buckhannon** who is listed on the 1789 personal property tax list of Bedford County.

Berkeley County
    William Buckhannon – wife and two children

    William Buckhannon is listed as doing nonmilitary service during the Revolutionary War. He was listed on a 1776 petition.

Brooke County
    William Buchanan – wife, seven children

    Born in Lancaster County, Pennsylvania in 1739, William Buchanan married Mary (McMullen) (born 1735, died 1797, Brooke County, Virginia). Brooke County later became a part of West Virginia. She died the same year as their 7th child was born. The family lived or owned land in several counties and most of the children appear to have been born in Monongalia County. William Buchanan died in 1814 in Ohio County.

Chesterfield County
    Neill Buchannan – wife, child and 24 slaves

    Neill Buchannan was born in 1742 in Chesterfield County. He served on the Committee of Correspondence at the beginning of the Revolutionary War. He was an heir in a 1789 will then appeared on the 1790 land tax list in both Chesterfield County and Prince George County where he also owned land.   He was also a slave owner and listed a runaway slave named Caesar in the Virginia Gazette of August 16, 1770. Neil married Mary (Gay). He died in 1797.

    Three other Buchanans appear in Chesterfield County in this time frame including **David Buchanan**, **James Buchanan** and **William Buchanan**.

    David Buchanan appears on both the Petersburg land tax list of 1790 and the personal property tax list of the same year.

James Buchanan is listed as a tenant living on rented land in 1790. He married Margaret (Gordon) in Petersburg in 1793.

William Buchanan appears on the 1790 land tax list.

Dinwiddie County
Andrew Buchanan – wife, one slave

Andrew Buchanan was a Fredericksburg attorney in the 1770s and was on the land tax list in both 1790 and 1800 and served as an executor of an estate in 1801. He sold his land to his brother-in-law in 1789, and eventually moved to Person County, North Carolina. He married Mary (Gentry). Andrew Buchanan had a slave named Lucky.

Fairfax County
Arthur Buchannan – wife and five children

Arthur Buchannan was born in Maryland in 1743. Arthur married Mary (Boswell) in 1762. He was a surveyor in Fairfax County in 1777 and appeared on the 1782 tax list of Fairfax County. He and his family later moved to North Carolina where he died in Yancy County in 1820.

Halifax County
James Buchannon – wife and four children

James Buchannon was listed in the 1782 Virginia tax census.

Henrico County
Alexander Buchanan - two slaves

Alexander Buchanan was a merchant in Richmond. He is listed as Buchannan in the 1790 personal property tax records. In the 1790s he had an indentured servant. He was a major securities investor in Richmond, speculated in land and made loans with collateral for slaves. There is a notice that he took a trip to New York and Philadelphia in 1792 and he was the executor of an estate in 1799. Robert Wright's book One Nation Under Debt[4] has more on Alexander Buchanan.

Alexandria Buchanan

Alexandria Buchanan was born about 1758. She is listed as the head of a family in Richmond's Ward 4 in 1788.

David Buchanan – wife, son, slaves

David Buchanan is listed at the birth of a child to one of his slaves in 1791. There is also a record of the death of his son, Silas, the next year. He was married to Elizabeth (Meriwether) in Prince George County in 1788. He is also listed as the power of attorney to sell the land and slaves of his brother Andrew, who was a resident of Glasgow, Scotland in 1788. He sold a slave, Jenny, to Richard Randolph in 1790.

James Buchanan – wife and 15 slaves

James Buchanan was a tobacco and salt merchant who was born about 1743. He served on the Committee of Correspondence for the county. He has accounts listed throughout the 1760s and 1770s. In the November 28, 1770 Virginia Gazette he advertised for three runaway slaves. He was an heir in a 1782 will. In 1788 he was listed among the Heads of Families of Richmond.

John Buchanan

John Buchanan was born in 1748 in Dumfries, Scotland, a half brother to James Buchanan. Arriving in Virginia in 1771, John did not want to be a merchant like his half-brother, so he returned to Scotland in 1775 to study theology and became a pastor of the Episcopal Church. He served various churches in Henrico County until 1785 when he became the rector of Henrico

Parish and minister at St. John's Church. In his position, he preached in Richmond during the 1780s and 1790s including services at the Virginia state capitol. In 1783 he posted a bond to perform marriages and also published a list of marriages he performed from 1785-1791. Listed as Buchannan in the 1790 personal property tax list, John Buchanan was a member of the Amicable Society of Richmond in the 1790s and 1800. He founded the Bible Society of Virginia in 1813. John Buchanan died in Richmond on December 22, 1822.

There also appears to be a second **John Buchanan** who owned ten slaves. Because there is no record of the minister owning slaves, it must be assumed there was a second resident of the same name.

Loudon County
Spencer Buchanan – wife, three children, two slaves

Spencer Buchannan was the son of William and Rachel (?) Buchanan. He married Elizabeth (Wigginton) and lived in Loudon County in 1790. In 1833 he was living in Kentucky where he died in 1840.

William Buchanan – two white males over 16, six slaves

William Buchanan was listed on the 1789 personal property tax list of Loudon County.

Monongalia County
William Buchannon

William Buchanan appears both on the land tax list of 1790 as well as a plaintiff in a slander suit in 1794. This was probably the William Buchanan from Brooke County because many of his children were born in Monongalia County.

Montgomery County – see Wythe County for persons who were living in that part of Montgomery County that became Wythe County in 1790.

Although not in the Reconstructed Census, there was a **Jeremiah Buckhannon** listed in Montgomery County.

Jeremiah Buckhannon was born in Benkers, Virginia in 1767. He married Sarah (Jones) in Franklin County, Virginia and the couple had 14 children. Jeremiah owned a house in 1792 and appears on the personal property tax list.

Ohio County
William I. Buchanan

William I. Buchanan was born in 1748/1750 in Cumberland County, Pennsylvania. He married Margaret (Morrison) (born 1753, Cumberland County, Pennsylvania, died 1786, Ohio County, Virginia) in 1773. The couple moved to Ohio County, (West) Virginia in 1775 and had children Archibald, Elizabeth, Jane, Mary, Sarah and Walter. He was executor of his father's will in York County, Pennsylvania in 1788. After 1800, William moved to Muskingum County, Ohio where he died in 1832.

Orange County
John Buchannon – three white males

Joshua Buchanan – three white males

Although most of their children were born in Baltimore, Maryland, Joshua Buchanan was supposedly born in 1741 in Scotland, the son of George and Eleanor (Rogers) Buchanan. He lived in both Orange and Spotsylvania Counties but is included here because he was listed on the 1790 personal property tax for Orange County. Joshua married and had children Henry, John, Thomas and William prior to 1790. He died in 1832.

Prince George County
Edward Buchanan

Edward Buchanan was listed on the 1790 property tax list for Prince George County.

Prince William County
John/Jno Buckanan

Robert Buchanan – one slave

Rockbridge County
Alexander Buchanan

James Buchanan

James Buchanan died in 1797 and his will was filed in June 1797. His will does not mention a wife or children.

James Patton Buchanan – three white males over 16

James Patton Buchanan was born in 1749 in Augusta County, Virginia. He served as a Captain, then Major in the Revolutionary War. James is listed as Buckhannan in the 1789 personal property tax and he appeared as a witness in a 1793 estate case. He married Isabel (Hall) (born 1735, Rockbridge County) in Botetourt County in 1763 and had 11 children, all born before the 1790 census. He died in Rockbridge County in 1808.

Spotsylvania County
James Buchanan

James Buchanan witnessed a deed in 1789.

Joshua Buckanan – one slave – see Orange County

Moses Buchanan – one slave

William Buchanan

William Buchanan was probably born in 1767, the son of Joshua Buchanan. He witnessed several wills and deeds in the county from 1790 to 1794. William married Effie (White) and moved to Kentucky where he died in Bourbon County.

Stafford County
Andrew Buchanan – 2 white males over 16, wife and daughter, 9 slaves

Andrew Buchanan lived in Falmouth, Stafford County. He made an indenture in 1772 and was listed as an Attorney at Law in Falmouth. He was an attorney in court cases in 1778. A Captain in the Revolution, he raised militia volunteers in Falmouth in 1776. In 1786 he bought 186 acres in Stafford County and appeared the next year on the county's personal property tax list. Andrew married first, a Miss Hewitt, and second, Anne (?). He had at least one daughter named Elizabeth who married in 1798. Andrew Buchanan died in Falmouth in 1804.

Surry County
Susanna Buchanan – six slaves

Susanna Buchanan first appears in the records as a witness to a 1782 will. She is listed in the 1782 local census with seven out dwellings and 10 slaves in the 1781 tax payer list and seven slaves in 1784. She then appears on both the 1790 land tax list and personal property tax list.

Washington County
Andrew Buchanan – wife

Andrew Buchanan was born in Chester County, Pennsylvania in 1732, son of Samuel and Martha Buchanan. In 1762 he married Joanna (Hay) (born 1742, died 1808, Davidson County, Tennessee) in Augusta County and had 12 children prior to the 1790 census. He served as a Major in the Revolutionary

War. He was listed in the county's 1787 and 1789 personal property tax records. He died on October 13, 1793 in Washington County. Many of his family moved to Tennessee.

Archibald Buchanan

Archibald Buchanan was born in 1730 in Chester County, Pennsylvania, the son of James and Martha (Allison) Buchanan. He moved with the family to Washington County in 1743. He married first, Nancy (Bowen) and had at least three children in the 1760s. After Nancy's death he married her sister, Agnes (Bowen) (McFerrin), a widow, and had another seven children. He served as a Sergeant in the Colonial Militia during the Revolutionary War. Even though he moved to Tennessee, he retained property in Washington County and was listed on the 1793 personal property tax list. He died in 1806 in Davidson, Tennessee. – *see also Trans-Appalachia*

Archibald Buchanan

The second Archibald Buchanan in Washington County was born in 1767, the son of John and Martha (Buchanan) Buchanan. He may still have been living with his parents in 1790. He married Martha (?) about 1801 and had nine children. He died in 1843 in Smyth County.

David Buchanan

The son of Andrew and Joanna (Hay) Buchanan, David Buchanan was born in Augusta County in 1764. He appears on the county's 1787 personal tax list. The next year he married Margaret (Steele) (born 1765, Augusta County, Virginia; died 1854, Lincoln County, Tennessee) in Rockbridge County and had five children. One of these children, Martha was born prior to 1790. David died in Lincoln County, Tennessee in 1844.

John Buchanan

The son of Samuel and Martha (Edmiston) Buchanan, John Buchanan was born in Augusta County in 1750. He married around 1775 and they had eight children, seven of whom were born prior to 1790. The family appears on the 1787 personal property tax record. John married a second time to Jane (Patterson) in Davidson County, Tennessee in 1792 and had five children between 1793 and 1802. John died in 1818 in Pulaski County, Arkansas. His will lists Jane Patterson and all the children by her. He also owned slaves as seen in the will which left slaves Sampson and Paul to his wife and the children of Poll to his daughter Munsy.

John Buchanan

This John Buchanan was born in Augusta County in 1745. He married Anne Ryburn (born 1762, Scotland, died 1829, Washington County) and had ten children. John died in 1824 in Washington County. Various genealogical sources differ on his year of birth, parentage and children.

Joseph Buchanan

Born in Ireland in 1743, Joseph Buchanan served in the Revolutionary War and received a land grant in 1785, the year he moved to Gladesprings, Washington County. He appears on the 1787 personal property tax list. He married Ann (Wilson) (born about 1770, died 1818, Washington County) and he had seven children that lived mainly in Smyth and Washington Counties. The children born prior to 1790 included David, Jane, John, Joseph and Samuel. One grandchild later moved to Arkansas. He died in 1816.

Matthew Buchanan – one white male over 16, wife

Born in 1762 in Augusta County, Matthew Buchanan was the son of Andrew and Joanna (Hay) Buchanan. He is listed on the 1787 personal property tax list. Matthew married Elizabeth (Edmondson) (born Augusta County, Virginia; died Washington County, Virginia) in 1780/1782 in Washington County. The couple had ten children, five born before 1790. The children born prior to the census included Andrew, Joana, Martha, Nancy and William. He died in 1831 in Washington County.

Moses Buchanan – one slave

Born in Augusta County in the 1740s, the son of Samuel and Martha (Edmiston) Buchanan, Moses Buchanan was listed on the 1787 personal property tax list in Washington County. Moses married Elizabeth (Harper) and had seven children. After Andrew Buchanan's death, he married the widow, Joanna (Hay) (Buchanan). He died in 1823.

Robert Buchanan – three slaves

Born in Augusta County in 1733, Robert Buchanan was the son of Samuel and Martha (Edmiston) Buchanan. He was a Captain of the Washington County militia during the Revolutionary War and fought Indians in Tennessee. He appeared on the personal property tax list in 1782, a jury list in 1783 and the 1787 land and personal property tax lists. He was also listed as selling land in 1778. Robert held three slaves named Peet, Poll and Sall. He married (?) and had five children. Robert died in Williamson County, Tennessee in 1818.

Samuel Buchanan – wife, one slave

Samuel Buchanan was born in 1748 in Augusta County, the son of Samuel & Martha (Keys) Buchanan. He appears on the county's 1782, 1789 and 1790 tax lists. He held a slave named Ellen as listed on the personal property tax lists. He married Elizabeth (Duncan) (born 1749, Augusta County, Virginia) in Augusta County in the 1760s and had eleven children, ten born before 1790, those being Andrew, Elizabeth, Jane, John, Martha,

Mary, Nancy, Petty(?), Robert and Samuel. Samuel died about 1835 in Washington County.

Wythe County

Alexander Buchanan

Born in 1728, Alexander Buchanan was the son of James and Martha (Allison) Buchanan. He served as a Lieutenant in the French and Indian Wars, 1752-1756, then held the same rank in the Militia in 1790. He was appointed a justice of the peace in 1786. He appeared on the 1782 tax list for Montgomery County but was in that part of the county that became Wythe County in 1790. He was also listed in the 1793 personal property tax list under the name Buchannon. He died 1798 in Wythe County. His will mentions his brothers John and Robert and children Alexander, John, Polley and William.

Jacob Buchannon

Jacob Buchanan appeared on the 1793 Wythe County personal property tax list.

James Buchanan, Sr. – five children

James Buchanan, Sr. the son of John and Elizabeth (Baxter) Buchanan. He served in the Virginia Militia from 1781 to 1784 and appears on the 1782 Montgomery County personal property tax list and the 1793 Wythe County list. His residence in 1790 was Wytheville and he had at least five children born prior to 1790.

James Buchanan, Jr.

James Buchanan was born in 1759 in Augusta County. He was listed in the 1793 personal property tax list. Before his death in 1816, he had nine children.

71

John Buchanan, Sr.

John Buchanan was born in Chester County, Pennsylvania in 1732, the son of James and Martha (Allison) Buchanan. He moved to Augusta County with his family in 1743. A weaver and farmer, he bought land in the 1750s including land in Beverly Manor, 1754. In 1769 he sold his land and in 1771 moved to Rich Valley, later a part of Smyth County. He gave land to his children between 1784 and 1806. He married Martha (Buchanan) (born 1738, daughter of John and Margaret (Campbell) Buchanan) in 1756 in Augusta County. He is listed on the 1790 and 1793 tax lists from Wythe County. His children born prior to 1790 include Alexander, Archibald, George, James, John and Patrick.

John Buchanan, Jr.

John Buchanan was listed in the 1790 land tax lists and the 1793 Wythe County personal property tax list.

Joseph Buchanan

Joseph Buchanan appeared on the 1793 Wythe County personal property tax list.

Nathaniel Buchanan

Nathaniel Buchanan was born in 1754, the son of John and Elizabeth (Baxter) Buchanan. He took the Oath of Allegiance in 1777 and fought with the Virginia troops including battles at Guilford Court House and Yorktown. He lived in Wytheville and was on the 1782 tax list in Montgomery County and the 1793 Wythe County tax list. He also was listed on a road order of 1785. Nathaniel had six children. Nathaniel moved to Kentucky in 1795 and died there in 1829.

Robert Buchanan/Buchannon – one slave

Born in Chester County, Pennsylvania in 1742, Robert Buchanan was the son of James and Martha (Allison). He moved with his family to Augusta County, Virginia in 1743. He served as a Captain in the Montgomery County Militia in 1777. He was an overseer of roads and is listed on road orders from 1785 and 1787 as well as the 1782 Montgomery County tax records. He sold land in Augusta County in 1792 and appeared in the 1790 land tax list and 1793 Wythe County personal property tax list. Robert married Margaret (McCutcheon) (b. 1759, Augusta County, d. 1789) and had at least five children. His will list his sons Alexander and John and three daughters.

York County – John Buchannon – one white male, one slave

John Buchannon is listed on the 1790 personal property tax list with one slave.

---

[1]*Baltimore: Past and Present with Biographical Sketches of Its Representative Men* (Baltimore, Richardson and Bennett, 1871).

[2]Lyman B. Chalkey, *Chronicles of the Scotch-Irish Settlement in Virginia, 1745 to 1800* (Rosslyn, Virginia: Commonwealth Printing Co., 1912). The three volume set is now in the public domain and available on Rootsweb.com.

[3]Augusta B. Fothergill and John Mark Naugle. *Virginia Tax Payers 1782-1787 Other Than Those Published by the United States Census Bureau.* (Baltimore, Marsyland: Genealogical Publishing Vo., 1940).

[4]Robert E. Wright, *One Nation Under Debt* (New York: McGraw Hill, 2008).

Chapter Four

DEEP SOUTH

While the states of the Deep South have often been considered as the premier slave states, this did not occur until after 1800. While South Carolina would later come to be viewed as the center of slavery in the 19th century, in 1790 the heart of slave country was further north in Maryland and Virginia.

The beginning of Southern settlement began in a contest between the Spanish and the English. Spanish movement north from Florida and English attempts to settle South Carolina resulted in conflict between the two nations. The Spanish incited Indian groups to attack the settlements of the Carolinas. In North Carolina from 1711 to 1713, and from 1711 to 1715 in South Carolina, Indians attempted to destroy the English settlements. At this time the Carolinas were united as a single Province of Carolina, which became a crown colony in 1719. Only after the Spanish realized that they were not going to be able to oust the English were the colonies able to flourish.

Once peace was established, the Province of Carolina grew until the two Carolinas were separated into separate colonies. The last of the colonies of the Deep South was Georgia, almost an afterthought as it was not begun until 1733, and that as an experiment by social reformers wanting to help ease the plight of those who had been involved in crime in England.

North Carolina

Roanoke, North Carolina was the site of the first attempted English settlement in North America in 1585. However, the settlement has become part of mystery and folklore as in 1588 it was found abandoned with only the word "Croatoan" scratched into a post. During the 1650s Virginians moved south to settle the land but it wasn't until 1705 that Bath was founded. Five years later New Bern and then other coastal settlements began in 1710.

As the colony grew, numbers of Scottish and Scotch-Irish immigrants arrived. The Scots settled the eastern seaboard while the Scotch-Irish moved into the interior and along the frontier. In the middle of the 1700s the governor of North Carolina encouraged Scottish immigration and provided a tax exemption for those who came from Scotland. Settling in the Upper Cape Fear region, these Scots maintained their own traditions throughout the 1700s. Many remained loyal to their homeland during the American rising against England. Several Loyalist units were formed including the North Carolina Highlanders. The first unit included 1,600 Highlanders who were defeated at Moore's Creek Bridge. In 1780 the unit was reformed with about 600 men who fought in the remainder of the war then left for Nova Scotia or Scotland. After the Revolution, when their land was confiscated for their loyalist support, many of these Scots and their families left the state and moved to Canada or the West Indies.

Migration from Pennsylvania and Virginia brought more Scotch-Irish settlers to the Appalachian regions of the colonies. As a result of the combined migration of both Scots and Scotch-Irish, North Carolina came to be the most "Scottish" state. Today it retains the highest percentage of Scots and Scottish lineage of any state.

North Carolina became a state in 1789 and the next year had a population of 393,751. In addition it had 100,783 slaves, the fourth most of the states.

Buchanans in North Carolina

The North Carolina counties with the highest percentage of Scotch-Irish also had the highest number of Buchanan families. As with the others of Scottish heritage, these people who escaped Scotland's wars with England often arrived in Pennsylvania and

Virginia then moved south into North Carolina. In a sense, the tide was just beginning as far more would come after 1790.

Most of North Carolina's Buchanan families of 1790 lived in the inland counties along the South Carolina border on a line running from Cumberland to Rutherford counties. None were located on the line of what became Tennessee except for those in Rutherford County. Later there would be a larger number who settled in the valleys of the Appalachian Mountains.

Caswell County
For some reason Caswell County census returns were blank for families whose last names began with the letters A to F. As a result the Buchanans listed here are simply the heads of household with no additional data in the census.

Andrew Buckhannon

Andrew Buchanan appeared in the 1777 state census and 1784 tax list. He was a buyer of items from an estate in 1787 and received estate payments in 1790.

James Buckhannon

Caswell County – Gloucester
John Buckhanan

John Buchanan is listed in several official records in North Carolina from 1786 to 1792. He purchased three slaves in 1786, paid a state fine to the treasurer in 1790/1791 and bought land in 1792. He married Catherine (Ledford) in 1799 and appeared in both the 1800 and 1810 censuses.

Craven County – New Bern
William Buchanan, one white male over age 16, three under 16, two females

Cumberland County – Fayette District
Hector Buchanan – one white male over age 16, one under 16, one female, seven slaves

Hector Rutherford Buchanan was appointed as a tax collector for four districts in 1791. He is mentioned in the 1801 will of his father-in-law and an 1802 estate. He married Ann Nancy (Campbell) in Cumberland Country and the couple had two children.

John Buchanan – three white males over 16, four under 16, three females

John Buchanan's family later moved to Tennessee.

Granville County
William Buckhannon – one white male over 16, one slave

William Buchanan was born in 1752 in Washington County, Virginia. He took the Oath of Allegiance in 1778 and married Sarah (Paschall) (born and died in Granville County). He had a daughter in 1793. William died in 1796 in Rockingham, North Carolina.

Although not listed in the official census count, **James Buchanan** was a county resident. He was on the county militia list in 1771 and took the Oath of Allegiance in 1778. He was a bond for the sale of land in 1770 and owned two parcels of land in 1778. In 1833 he signed an affidavit for Joseph Pittman to receive a pension for Revolutionary War service.

Guilford County – Salisbury District
James Buchanan – two white males over 16, three females

James Buchanan was a tavern keeper in 1782. He bought and sold land from 1783 to 1787 and was an administrator or creditor of several estates in the 1780s. Court records also mention a lot owned by him in 1783. He appears in the 1800 census as well.

Lincoln County – Morgan District
Thomas Buccannon – one white male over 16, two under 16, four females

Born in 1748 in York County, Pennsylvania, Thomas Buchanan fought in the Revolutionary War and migrated from Pennsylvania to North Carolina. In 1775 he married Martha (Newton) (born 1754, York County, Pennsylvania; died 1830, Rutherford County, North Carolina). He had ten children of which Elizabeth, James, Jane, Martheu (Patsy?), Mary, Thomas and William were born prior to 1790. He died in North Carolina in 1807. Some of his descendants moved to Arkansas and Missouri.

Mecklenburg County – Salisbury District
James Bucannon – one white male over 16, three females

James Buchanan was listed on the tax list in Cpt. Hood's Company. He bought land in the 1790s and had a mortgage in 1800. He also appeared in the 1800 census.

Robert Buckhanon – three white males over 16, two under 16, four females

Robert Buchanan lived in the county through at least 1820 as seen in the various census records.

Samuel Buckhannon – three white males over 16, two under 16, two females

Born in 1726 in Lancaster, County, Pennsylvania, the son of Samuel Buchanan, this Samuel Buchanan served in several official positions in Mecklenburg County. He was appointed constable from 1783 to 1787, and served on several juries in the

1790s, including a grand jury in 1796. He sold land to James Buchanan in 1795. Samuel married Barbara (?) and had nine children. The family moved to York County, South Carolina in 1799, where Samuel died in 1801.

A Mecklenburg county taxables list for Cpt. Hood's Company also includes **John Buchanan, Sr.** with 30 acres, **John Buchanan, Jr.** and **James Buchanan** with a notation of "(black)" after his name, which might indicate he was a freedman of color.

Moore County – Fayette District
John Buchannan – two white males over 16, two under 16, two females

Margery Buchannan – one white male under 16, one female

Randolph County – Hillsborough District
William Buckhannon – single white male

William Buchanan fought in the Revolutionary War and his descendants received his pension because William died before 1832 when the pension was issued.

Richmond County – Fayette District
John Buchannan – one white male over 16, one female

John was born in Scotland while his wife, Sarah, was born in North Carolina.

William Buchannan – two white males over 16, one under 16, six females

William, Buchanan also appears in the 1810 census. His will was probated in the county in 1818.

Robeson County – Fayette District
   Peter Buchannan – two white males over 16, three under 16, two females

   Peter Buchanan married Mary (McMillan). He purchased land in 1803 as evidenced by county deed records. In the 1810 census he is listed with a family of four white males over 16, one under 16, two females and seven slaves.

Rockingham County – Salisbury District
   William Buckanon – two white males over 16, four under 16, four females

   There is much confusion in genealogical sources about William Buchanan and his family. Some say he was born in 1735, others in 1752. Many say he was born in County Tyrone, Ireland, the son of John and Jane (Russell) Buchanan, while others deny it.

   What is certain is that county records show that William married Catherine (McCaleb) (born in Guilford County, North Carolina; died 1835) in Guilford County. William died in 1795 in Rockingham County. Some of his descendants moved to Alabama, South Carolina and Texas.

Rutherford County – Morgan District
   James Buccannon – three white males over 16, two females

   James Buchanan moved to Rutherford County around 1760. He is listed on a 1772 deed and appears on the county's 1782 tax list. He married Elizabeth (Willis) (born 1734, Charles County, Maryland; died 1792, Rutherford County) in 1760 in Virginia. He was a bondsman for his son, Joseph's, wedding. He is listed in the Burke County, North Carolina census of 1800 and he died in Burke County.

Sampson County – Fayette District
James Buchannan – three white males over 16, two females, one slave

South Carolina

When DeSoto explored the American Southeast in 1540, he entered part of what would later be South Carolina. This established a Spanish claim to the land. Yet the Spaniards in Florida did little to settle the region. When the English arrived, the Spanish colonial government opposed them. Unlike in North Carolina, where no large active effort was made to drive the English out, the Spanish were much more active in South Carolina. Armed Spanish forces would occasionally attack English settlements and the Spanish armed Indians to attack the settlements. Because of this the original attempts to settle the province failed until 1670 when the first lasting settlement was established near modern Charleston. Ten years later the settlement was moved to the current location of the modern city. Planters and their slaves from Barbados settled into the area after 1670 and around 1700 French Huguenots arrived in the Province. Due to the colony's religious tolerance, Jews came to South Carolina as well.

Following the Indian Wars which lasted from 1711-1715, South Carolina grew slowly. It was separated from North Carolina in 1729 when the Province of Carolina was divided in two. Settlement away from the coastal regions was slow to begin and didn't really blossom until 1755. The upland or inland settlements grew mainly through the migration of Scotch-Irish and poor British immigrants. Yet by the time of the Revolution, South Carolina was among the richest of the British colonies due to its rice, indigo and slave trade.

When the British established the Townsend Acts to tax American goods, the colony joined Massachusetts in open opposition. Once war began, South Carolina declared its independence months before the American Declaration of

Independence was issued. Outright war evaded the colony for a time. Although the British failed in an attempt to take Charleston in 1776, in 1780 they returned, defeated the American army after a siege of Charleston and seized the coastal regions of the colony. As with other colonies, Loyalists supported the British and fought alongside them. The Cherokee Indians sided with the British and made war on the frontier settlements.

The Americans fought a guerilla war against the occupying British and the British struck back at civilian populations. It is said that there were more battles fought in South Carolina during the Revolution than in any other state, despite the fact that the British did not come until later in the war. In the end the British and their allies were defeated and the remainder of the British left South Carolina in 1782 followed by many of the Loyalists.

By 1790, South Carolina was an American state and that year the government moved from Charleston to the new state capital, Columbia. Its population was 249,073 which included a slave population of 107,094. While the state had the second highest total slave population, it had the highest percentage of slaves in the total population of any state, with approximately 48.3% of the population being slaves.

Buchanans in South Carolina

The great majority of the Buchanan families in the 1790 census were located in the Scotch-Irish areas in the Ninety-Six District. A few were in counties in the Camden District but only one family is listed in the eastern part of the state, that being in Charleston.

Abbeville
James Bochanon – three white males over 16, four white females

James Buchanan was listed in the plat maps for 1784-1787 as well as in the land records in the 1790s. he married Mary Frances (Arnold) and had four children. He died in 1805 and his will, probated in the county, mentions his wife and children Frances, Mary, Rebecca and Robert as well as a plantation.

Jno Bochanon – one white male over 16, two under 16, four females

Jonathan Buchanan is mentioned in the plat map book for 1784-1787.

Mary Bochanon – three females

Mary Buchanan was born in Ireland and was an immigrant in the second wave of Scotch-Irish immigration in 1776/1777. She died in 1796. In her will, proved in 1797, Mary mentions some of her children, including George, Henry, James, John, Margaret, Mary, Robert and William.

William Bochanon – one white male over 16, two under 16, two females

William Buchanan was born about 1762 in Ireland. He came to the United States in 1768. During the Revolutionary War he served nine different times and fought at Cowpens. He was captured at the Battle of Kettle Creek. After the war, William was appointed justice of the peace in 1783. He owned lands that were listed in the 1784-1787 plat book. William married Polly (Morrow) and had eight or nine children. He died in 1836.

Camden
Benjamin Buchanan

Benjamin Buchanan owned two plats of land recorded in the 1784-1787 plat maps. As there is no family listed, he may be the same person that lived in the Newberry District but only owned land in the Camden District.

James Buchannon – two white males over 16, three females

James Buchannon – one white male over 16, one under 16, one female

Jno Buchanan – one white male over 16, two under 16, five females

John Buchanan – one white male over 16, one under 16, three slaves

This may be the same man who lived in Fairfield County and who bought land in the Camden District in 1786.

Charleston – St. James Santee Parish
John Buchannon – one white male over 16, five females, 25 slaves

Born in 1725, John Buchanan was a physician. He served as a surgeon and Captain of the South Carolina Line in 1781-1782. He married Elizabeth (?) (born 1764, died 1802). John was listed as an executor of an estate in 1794. He was also in the county's 1800 census.

Chester County
John Buckanan – two white males over 16, one under 16, five females

Fairfield County
John Buchanan – one white male over 16, one female, three slaves

Born in Ireland about 1750, John Buchanan arrived in South Carolina in the 1770s. He served in the Cherokee Wars and was a Captain of the 1st and 6th South Carolina Line during the Revolution. He was captured in May 1780, exchanged in June 1781 and became Captain of the 3rd Regiment in 1782-1783, being brevetted Major in 1783. After the war he farmed and opened an inn listed as a "house of entertainment." In Winnsboro he was one of the builders of the Methodist Church. He was also a witness to a will in 1813. He married Sallie (Burney) (Milling) but had no children. His black servant, Fortune, is noted in a number of accounts of John Buchanan's activities. John Buchanan died in Winnsboro in 1824.

Creighton Buchanan – one white male over 16, one under 16, one female

Although not listed in the census, **Creighton Buchanan** was a resident of Fairfield County in 1790 according to <u>History of Fairfield County, South Carolina</u>[1] and other sources.

Creighton Buchanan was born in Antrim, Northern Ireland in 1760, the son of John and Rachel (Phillips) Buchanan. In 1789 he moved to Little River, South Carolina and settled in Fairfield County on his brother-in-law's land. In 1805 he moved to Winnsboro and in 1807 he bought his brother's tavern. Creighton Buchanan married Mary (Milliken) and they couple had six children, of which John was born in 1790. Creighton Buchanan died in December 1824. One of his sons moved to Texas.

Greenwood
William Buchanan

William Buchanan was born in Ireland in 1762 and died in Greenwood County in 1842. He served as a Private in Picken's Regiment during the Revolutionary War and was captured by the British at Kettle Creek in 1778. He also served in several South Carolina regiments fighting Indians and the British at Cowpens. But during the war and after, his residence was at Cambridge, Greenwood County. After the war he worked on local roads in the 1780s. He married Polly (?) and had several children.

Lancaster County

James Buchanan – one white male over 16, one under 16

James Buchanan – one white male over 16, one under 16, three females

Newberry District (County)

Ben Buckhannan – one white male over 16, two under 16, two females

Born in Prince William County, Virginia in 1754, Benjamin Buchanan was the son of John and Mary (Ross) Buchanan. He served as a Private and then a served as a Corporal in 1st and 6th South Carolina Line during the Revolutionary War. He married Mary (Wood) and had 14 children. He later moved to Jasper County, Georgia where he died in 1821.

George Buckhannan – two white males over 16, one female

George Buchanan was a Corporal in the 6th South Carolina Line in 1777 and a Sergeant in 1778. He was captured in May 1780 when the British captured Charleston and was held as a prisoner at Sullivan's Island. After the war he lived in the Newberry District until the 1790s when he moved to Marion County, Georgia and appears in the 1800 census there.

James Buckhannan – two white males over 16, three over 16, two females, one slave

James Buchanan was still living in the District at the time of the 1800 census.

John Buckhannan – three white males over 16, one female, seven slaves

John Buchanan was born in 1720 in Middlesex County, Virginia, the son of Joseph and Elizabeth (Neville) Buchanan. In 1740 he married Elizabeth (Haynie) (born 1725, Northumberland County, Virginia; died 1805, Newberry County) in Prince William County, Virginia. He died in 1793 and his will listed his wife and children Anna, Jesse, John, Mary, Micajah, Nancy, Susannah and William. A local census states that in 1790 John Buchanan had nine slaves rather than the seven reported by the federal census. As detailed in his will, at his death he held 14 slaves.

John Buckhannan, Jr. – one white male over 16, one under 16, two females

John Buchanan, Jr. was born in 1742 in Prince William County, Virginia, the son of John and Elizabeth (Haynie) Buchanan. In the Newberry District he witnessed deeds in 1783 and 1787. He married Janet (Ross) (born about 1765) and had a son, Alexander. John Buchanan, Jr. died in Winnsboro in 1824.

Joseph Buckhannan -one white male over 16, one female

This Joseph Buchanan was probably the son of Joseph and Elizabeth (Neville) Buchanan who moved from Prince William County, Virginia to the Newberry District..

Micajah Buchanan

Born in Prince William County, Virginia in 1746, Micajah Buchanan was the son of John and Elizabeth (Haynie) Buchanan. Micajah married Jane (?) (born about 1750). He died in 1793 in the Newberry District.

Pendleton District (County)
Thomas Buckhanan – one white male over 16, three under 16, two females

Thomas Buchanan served in the South Carolina Militia in 1781-1782. He was still in the county in the 1800 census but moved to Tennessee where he received his Revolutionary War pension in 1831.

Union County
  Col. James Buchannan – one white male over 16, one under 16, one Female

  William Buckhannan – three white males over 16, one under 16, five females, three slaves

  Born in Prince William Buchanan, Virginia in 1752, William Haynie Buchanan was the son of John and Elizabeth (Haynie) Buchanan. He was a witness to various wills in the 1780s and was with the county commissioners in 1783 when they named Buchanan Creek. He served as an executor in a 1791 estate and a delegate to his church association in 1792. He married Frances (Stribling) (born 1756, Prince William County, Virginia; died 1818, Newberry District, South Carolina) in 1774 in the Newberry District. William Haynie Buchanan died after 1820 in Lawrence County, Tennessee. Some of his descendants lived in Tennessee and Mississippi.

York County – **Jno Buchanan** – one white male over 16, two under 16, five females

Georgia

  The last of the Deep South states in 1790 was Georgia. It was a land of conflict between Spanish, British and Indian nations. The Spanish established missions in a variety of coastal sites but Governor Moore of South Carolina drove them out in the early 1700s. South Carolina then used Indian allies to attack the Spanish and their allies, enslaving Indians from enemy nations. In the meantime, Scottish traders from the Carolinas opened a trading post with the Indians in 1690.

Following the Indian wars, John Oglethorpe, an advocate for prison reform, was granted permission to establish a colony in Georgia. In 1733, six ships landed at the site of modern Savannah to begin the permanent colonization of Georgia. Two years later a royal charter was issued for Georgia. The charter prohibited slavery in Georgia, but this was overturned in 1750. In addition, liquor was prohibited.

Georgia was among the smallest of the states when it entered the United States. Although there were a number of soldiers from the American forces that settled in Georgia after the Revolution, its population remained small during the 1700s. By 1790 its population was only about 56,100 as estimated by the Census Bureau, the second smallest state when excluding the slave population. Unlike other small states, Georgia had an estimated slave population of 29,264, which was more than half the number of the non-slave population.

The census figures are uncertain because Georgia was one of the states for which the census records were either burned or lost. As a result, the reconstructed census[1] and other local records must be used in looking at the population of 1790.

Although there was early Scottish trade in Georgia, there was never a large permanent Scottish presence in the colony's early years. Dutch religious refugees and English debtor prisoners were among the early Georgian settlers. Later settlement included the Scotch-Irish who continued to migrate down from Pennsylvania and Virginia through the Carolinas, although in Georgia they settled near the coast because the vast lands of the Cherokee Nation were in central and western Georgia.

Buchanans in Georgia

Several of the Buchanans in 1790 Georgia were in families headed by veterans of the Revolutionary War. Land

90

grants were issued between 1783 and 1787 to some of the former soldiers while others moved from other states prior to 1790.

Baldwin County
George H. Buchanan

Born in 1759, George H. Buchanan lived in the part of Baldwin County that would later become Jasper County. He served as a Sergeant in the South Carolina Militia and was on the 1835 pension list and the 1840 census for Marion County, Georgia. He died in 1845 in Marion County.

Robert Buchannan

Robert Buchanan moved to Georgia from Kentucky in the 1780s with his wife Sarah (Wilson) and 9 children Gwen (?), John, Martha, Mary, Nancy, Patience, Robert, Samuel and Thomas. His will abstract lists his wife Sarah and both of their wills appear in the later Index of Wills for Baldwin County, 1806-1819. He died in 1809 in Baldwin County and she died in 1825.

Elbert County
Ebenezer Buchanan

Listed as Abanezer, this man purchased land in Elbert County in 1790.

Jno Buchanan

John Buchanan witnessed deeds in 1791 and 1817.

Greene County
Jno Buchanan

Born about 1736 in Virginia, John Buchanan moved to Mecklenburg County, North Carolina in 1758, then Georgia in 1773. He appears to have been living in Wilkes County in 1790 but in Greene County at the time of his death in 1801. He served in the South Carolina Militia fighting at Kettle Creek. John was a tailor by profession. He and his wife are listed in the 1784-1785 Wilkes County deed book for both selling and buying land in 1785. The 1785 Little River Land Surveys list John Buchanan.[2] In Wilkes County Deed Book DD, a listing shows that in 1789 he also sold land and was a witness to another deed. He is also listed with a wife, two daughters , an indentured servant and 150 acres in that county. John married Ann (?) in 1750 and had five children, James, John, Joseph, Sarah and William, all born in North Carolina.

Joseph Buchanan

The son of John and Ann (?) Buchanan, Joseph Buchanan was born in North Carolina and died in Morgan County, Georgia in 1810.

Richmond County
James Buckanan

James Buchanan was born in 1760, possibly in North Carolina. He was a secretary recording marriages in Richmond County in the 1790s. He married Jane (Chambers) in Richmond County, Georgia in 1797, probably his second marriage as he had John, Joseph and Margaret prior to 1790. He had a total of 16 children.

Joseph Buchanan

William Buchanan

Not only was William Buchanan in the reconstructed census but his name is found on local records including a petition to the Governor.

Wilkes County
Joseph Buchanan/Buckhanan

Joseph Buchanan was born in 1762 and moved to Georgia prior to the Revolution. He served as a Private of Georgia troops during the war and received land grants for his service. Joseph Buckhannon was listed on the 1791 tax list for the Clay District. He eventually moved to Louisiana where he died in 1811.

_____

[1]Marie De LaMar and Elisabeth Rothstein. *The Reconstructed Census of Georgia* (Baltimore: Genealogical Publishing Co., 1985).

[2]Grace Gilliam Davidson, comp., "The Ceded Lands," *Early Records of Georgia, vi, Wilkes County.* (Macon, Georgia, 1933), 19.

Chapter Five

TRANS-APPALACHIA

The United States of 1790 extended beyond the inhabited coastal regions of the 13 colonies. Settlers had crossed the Appalachian Mountains into the extended territories of Pennsylvania, Virginia, North Carolina and Georgia. Two official territories existed beyond the Appalachians. In 1787 the Northwest Territories was created to include the land that would later become the states of Ohio, Illinois, Indiana, Michigan and Wisconsin, and even a small slice of what is now the northeastern part of Minnesota. To create this territory, the states of New England, New York, Pennsylvania and Virginia ceded their rights to the federal government.

Similarly, the Southwest Territory was created in 1790 to include the land south of the Ohio River. Yet the designation eventually applied only to Tennessee until its admittance to the United States in 1796. While Tennessee came from territory ceded by North Carolina after the Revolutionary War, Kentucky had essentially broken off from the Virginia claims in 1790 and was admitted to the Union in 1792 after Virginia agreed to give up its claim.

The census recognized these areas by counting people in certain districts west of the Appalachian Mountains. As with several other areas, the 1790 census data for these "western" districts was either destroyed by the British when they burned Washington, D.C. during the War of 1812 or lost by the state governments, depending on which view is correct. The end result is the same, however, so to review the Buchanans in 1790 requires that the reconstructed censuses be examined for these trans-Appalachian areas. Even then, it is probable that in some areas, there were other families not listed because the reconstructed data was usually based on land tax information and would not cover tenant families.

Ancestry.com, probably the largest collection of census data on the Internet, has the reconstructed census data for the three trans-Appalachian districts in 1790. Kentucky's reconstructed data based on taxpayer lists may also be found on the Adair County Rootsweb site.

Districts in 1790 Census

The districts included in the 1790 census were from the modern states of Ohio, Kentucky and Tennessee. Although none of these areas were yet states, and settlements existed outside the bounds of these current states, the census did not reach further west. Vincennes in Indiana, and both Cahokia and Kaskaskia, as well as smaller settlements that existed prior to 1783, became part of the Northwest Territories after the Revolutionary War. Technically, in 1790 Illinois had two counties established, that of St. Clair and Knox, and a Congressional Committee in 1788 found families in not only Cahokia and Kaskaskia but also Prairie du Rocher and Fort Chartres and St. Philippe in the Illinois area of the Northwest Territories. Yet only one part of the Northwest Territories, that of Ohio, would be among those areas in which the census took place.

Kentucky was the earliest settled of the three census districts. In 1774 James Harrod established Harrodsburg, but Indians drove the settlers out until 1775. During 1775, Boonesborough, Boiling Springs, Lexington and St. Asaph were all established. Around 1778, Louisville was founded and Virginia recognized the city charter in 1780. One of the first explorers, Daniel Boone first moved through the Cumberland Gap in 1775 and by 1790 there was a road wide enough to handle wagons going through the gap. It was estimated by the Census Bureau that there were 45,000 people in Kentucky by 1780 and approximately 74,000 in 1790. In addition, in 1790 Kentucky had 12,430 slaves according to the Census Bureau estimate. Ironically, Daniel Boone eventually moved on to Missouri, allegedly because Kentucky had become too crowded.[1]

96

Settlement in Ohio had begun by 1790 and several towns had been formed. Although Fort Steuben was established in 1786, the settlement around the fort did not become a city until 1797. The settlers of the time were essentially squatters from other areas. The Jefferson County Historical Society indicates that even though the fort later burned down, there remained a cluster of homes around it. In 1797 this would become the city of Steubenville.

The claim to being the first city founded in Ohio revolves around three settlements all established in 1788. The apparent first permanent settlement in Ohio was at Marietta in modern Washington County, Ohio, when mainly Scottish, Irish, Connecticut and Massachusetts veterans of the Revolution moved west.

Also in 1788, Columbia in modern Hamilton County was established by New Jersey settlers. Losantville, established in December 1788 by other New Jersey settlers, was renamed two years later by Governor St. Clair and became modern Cincinnati. The next year a third settlement at North Bend was created by New Jersey residents. This was later the birthplace and home of two American presidents, William Henry Harrison and Benjamin Harrison. Gallipolis was established in 1790 by French immigrants.

For Tennessee, settlement began later and at a slower pace due to the native population in the South. Although the Southwest Territory was created in 1790, maps of it show that much of the southern part of the modern state was comprised on\f Native American lands. Only three counties had been established by 1790, but the Census Bureau estimated that they contained about 36,000 residents.

Due to internal conflict in North Carolina, refugees from the Regulator War began arriving in the area in the 1770s. Settlers already were living in modern Elizabethton by 1772, and Easton's Station followed shortly thereafter. Nashville, originally known as Buchanan's Station, was founded in 1779. Some historians indicate that John Robertson and a group of followers established Nashville, but others state that Major John Buchanan, his wife Sally, and other family members established the original station in 1779 before the Robertson party arrived. Whichever is correct, the Buchanans were heavily involved with the community, however, and during the 1781 Battle of the Bluffs with the Indians, Alexander Buchanan of the settlement was killed. John Buchanan's first wife died and he married (Sarah) Sally Ridley around 1790. John Buchanan was also known for publishing the first book in Tennessee in 1781.

Although past the 1790 census, the Battle at Buchanan's Station occurred on September 30, 1792 when a variety of Indian groups tried to dislodge the Nashville settlers, numbering around 60. While the original structure is now gone, a historical sign now marks the site. Not only did the settlers drive back the Indians during the battle, but several Indian leaders were killed, including the brother of Tecumseh. It also ended the attempt by the Spanish to arm the Indians to wipe out settlement in the American territories.

Buchanans in Trans-Appalachia, 1790

In each of the districts enumerated in the reconstructed census data for 1790, Buchanans were present. Kentucky, Ohio and Tennessee each had several families which were counted, and others that were missed. Because Tennessee's population was more compactly located in a few areas, it would have been easier to locate the families as opposed to the three distinct areas of settlement in Ohio distant from each other or the wider variety of settlements in Kentucky.

Buchanan families were found in several **Kentucky** counties according to taxpayer data and local sources.

Bourbon County – James Buchanon/Buckhanon

James Buchanan was listed on the 1790 Bourbon County tax list. He was probably the same person that signed a petition in Bourbon County in 1787.

Lincoln County – William Bachenan

William Buchanan was listed on the April 3, 1790 tax list for Lincoln County.

Mason County – Alexander Buckhannon

Alexander Buchanan was listed as a property owner on the June 23, 1790 Mason County tax list. The <u>History of Clermont County</u>[2] states that Alexander moved to Maysville, Mason County, in 1790, then to Germantown, then to Clermont County, Ohio in1795 or 1796. This Alexander, who was born in Scotland and came to America in 1764 lived in Washington County, Pennsylvania prior to moving to Kentucky. He was a Revolutionary War veteran. Alexander married Margaret (Shed) and the couple had eight children. Information on their son, William, indicates he lived in Kentucky from, 1789 to 1795 then moved to Clermont County, Ohio, in 1795. Alexander purchased land in Clermont County in 1801 and died in 1803. Both he and Margaret are buried in the Calvary Cemetery in Clermont County.

James Buchanan

James Buchanan appears on the 1790 tax list of Mason County.

Woodford County – Alexander Buchanan

It is sometimes amazing how many different genealogies exist for the same person but with differing information. So it is with this Alexander Buchanan and one of his wives, Rachel Van Schaik (and various other spellings due to Dutch background).

Genealogical sources on the Internet vary widely on information regarding this family. Some genealogies list him as born in New York while others list his birth in New Jersey. Some have him living in a few places, moving from New Jersey to Kentucky then Ohio while others have him living in several southern states before landing in Kentucky then Ohio. Some list him as a relative of President Buchanan while others do not. Some list children born in Wythe County, Virginia, which didn't exist until 1790, while others list the latter children as born in Kentucky. Some have his death in Kentucky while others correctly list it in Ohio.

Making matters more unusual, there were at least two Alexander Buchanans and their families that moved to Kentucky about the same time then moved to Clermont County, Ohio in the 1790s. A third Alexander Buchanan family is also listed in Clermont County in the early 1800s, but appears to be the son of one of the other Alexanders. One of the two often confused Alexander Buchanans was born in Scotland, while the other was born in America. One died in 1803 and the other in 1824. Many of the children had similar names. The book Clermont County, Ohio, 1980 gives a brief biography of each Alexander Buchanan and family.

It appears that the Alexander Buchanan of Woodford County was born in New York or New Jersey. It is known that he married Rachel VanSchaik (or variations of name) in Passaic, New Jersey in 1772. He fought with Capt. Tucker's Company of the 1st New Jersey Line during the Revolutionary War. Some of his descendants claim he was captured, then escaped, from the British. The reference to living in Virginia may be that, after 1782, he had children born in the part of Virginia that became Kentucky. At least two of these were born in Woodford County. Because Kentucky was among the Trans-Appalachia districts in 1790 and has no remaining census data, one must use the reconstructed census which puts Alexander and his family in Woodford County. He appears there on tax lists during the mid-1790s.

Alexander Buchanan and his family moved to Clermont County, Ohio around 1799. This Alexander Buchanan died in Clermont County, Ohio in 1824.

George Buchanon

It is believed that George Buchanan was born in Ireland, then migrated to York County, Pennsylvania in 1774. He served as Private in the 4th Pennsylvania Line during the Revolution. He apparently moved to Kentucky about 1790 or 1791, appearing in the Woodford County, Kentucky tax rolls from 1792-1795. The specific genealogy of this man is confused because of differing and altered genealogies from the past.

Other Kentucky

According to the Rock Valley Family History Collection, 1st series, **Victor Buchanan** was born in 1762 in Lancaster County, Pennsylvania. He first married Elizabeth (Allison) (died 1795, Kentucky) in July 1790 in York County, then moved to Port William, Kentucky at about the same time. He does not appear in the Pennsylvania census of 1790, so he may have moved or been moving to Kentucky at the time. His three children by Elizabeth were born in Kentucky, the first in 1793. He married a second time to Rebekah (Tucker) (born 1775, Shelby, Kentucky, died 1848, Lawrence County, Illinois) in 1799 in Kentucky and had four more children by her. In 1819 he moved to Gallatin County, Kentucky, then eventually to Lawrence County, Illinois where he died in 1843.

Ohio – John Buchanan

In Ohio, John Buchanan was one of the settlers who crossed into the Northwest Territory in 1785 and settled around Fort Steuben.[3] He was born in Londonderry, Ireland, of Scotch-Irish descent and moved to Pennsylvania. After serving in the American Revolution, he moved across the Ohio River. Once the Treaty of Greenville was signed in 1795 and formerly Indian land could legally be purchased in Ohio, John purchased property in Jefferson County. He is mentioned again as the fifer at Steubenville's July 4, 1826 celebration of the 50th anniversary of the Declaration of Independence.

Tennessee

Because the Buchanans were instrumental in founding Nashville, they were noticeable in the 1790 reconstructed Tennessee census. There were also other Buchanans that migrated from western parts of Virginia into the new territory in the 1780s.

Davidson County - Archibald Buchanan,

The son of James and Martha (Allison) Buchanan, Archibald Buchanan was born in Pennsylvania in 1728. He lived in Augusta County, Virginia after his family moved there in 1743. In 1782 he was on the Augusta County tax list. According to Tennessee Records[4], he moved to Donelson, Davidson County and was on the 1787 tax roll of Davidson County. A weaver by trade, in Donelson he built his mansion, "Old Blue Brick" where he was buried after his death in 1806. His tombstone indicates he fought as a Private with the Virginia Line in the Revolution. As a result of his military service, he received a Virginia land grant from his service in Captain Preston's Rangers during the French and Indian War and possibly others after his service in the Revolutionary War. In 1789 he bought additional land in Davidson County. He married Nancy (Bowen) (died 1759, Augusta County) in the 1750s in Augusta County. Two years after her death he married Agnes (Bowen) (born 1734, Virginia; died 1803, Nashville, Tennessee). After her death he married Patsy (Motney) in1803. Archibald died in 1806.

James Buchanan was born in 1763, the son of Archibald and Agnes (Bowen) Buchanan. He was a signer of the Cumberland Compact in 1780 and moved with his parents to

102

Donelson, Davidson County in 1785. About 1810 he married Lucinda (East) and had 16 children.

Major John Buchanan was born in 1759 in Harrisburg, Pennsylvania, the son of John and Jane (Trindle) Buchanan. His family moved to Guilford Courthouse in North Carolina in 1770, the Danville, Kentucky in 1774. In 1778/1779, the family moved to Tennessee prior to his father's death in the Indian battles of 1787-1788. Along with Major John Buchanan came his brothers Alexander, who was killed by Indians in 1781, and Samuel, killed by Indians in 1787. Major John Buchanan's name was on the 1787 tax roll, a deed purchasing land in 1788 and he served on the first Davidson County grand jury duty the same year. It was his station that was attacked in 1792. He married first, Margaret (Kennedy) in 1786 and she died in childbirth. He married again in October 1791 in Nashville to Sarah (Ridley) (born 1774, died 1831) and they had 13 children. It was Sarah Ridley Buchanan who became the heroine of the battle at Buchanan's Station. John Buchanan died the year after Sarah in 1831 in Nashville.

Moses Buchanan was born about 1750 and died in 1823.

The son of James and Martha (Allison) Buchanan, **Robert Buchanan** was born in 1733. He married Mary (?) (born Augusta County, Virginia; d. Williamson County, Tennessee) in Augusta County, Virginia. The couple sold their land in Augusta County in 1765 but it is uncertain where they moved. They may have moved first to Davidson County, Tennessee but were in Williamson County by the early 1800s. Their daughter Martha, who was married to Thomas Edmiston, moved to Tennessee in 1782. Robert Buchanan died in 1818in Williamson County.

Encyclopedia of World Biography and other Kentucky sources found at Ancestry.com.

The History of Clermont County. (Philadelphia: Everts, 1880), 367.

[3]Joseph B. Doyle, *Twentieth Century History of Steubenville and Jefferson County* (Chicago: Richmond-Arnold Publishing Co., 1910), 109.

[4] *Tennessee Records*, v. 1, 126, 261.

NAME INDEX

This index is arranged alphabetically so that some names appear out of order because of the addition of "Jr" "Sr" and the like. Also, because state abbreviations vary from the order in which the states spelled out appear, there are some variations, such as NC appearing before NJ or NY.

Buchanans by Various Spellings

Bachenan

William (KY)...99

Bochanon

Frances (SC)......................84	Mary (SC)................................74
George (SC)......................84	Mary Francis (Arnold) (SC)............84
Henry (SC).......................84	Polly (Morrow) (SC)....................84
James (SC)..................83, 84	Rebecca (SC)............................84
Jno (SC)..........................84	Robert (SC)..............................84
John (SC..........................84	William (SC)............................84
Margaret (SC)....................84	

Bucannon

George (PA).....................34	Marey (PA)...............................34
James (NC)......................79	

Buccannon

Elizabeth (NC).................79	Martha (Newton) (NC)................79
Elizabeth (Willis) (NC).......81	Martheu (Patsy?) (NC)................79
James (NC)..................79, 81	Mary (NC).............................79
Jane (NC).......................79	Thomas (NC)..........................79
Joseph (NC)...................81	William (NC)..........................79

Bucchannon

James Bucchannon (PA)........37

Buchanan

Abraham (NJ)....................21	Alexander (PA)............30, 32, 34
Agnes (Bowen) (McFerrin) (VA)	Alexander (SCOT)....................15
...........................68, 102	America (Copenhaver) (VA)..........59
Alexander (KY, OH)......99-101.	Alexander (VA)...57, 60, 62-63, 66,
Alexander (KY, NC, PA, TN)...	71-73
...............................103	Alexander (VT).......................,,...5
Alexander (MD)................49	Alexander Pitt (MD, VA)..........48-49
Alexander (NY)................ 16	Alexandria (VA).......................63
Alexander (OH)..............100	Andrew (MD)......................47, 49

108

Catherine (McCaleb) (NC)...81
Arter (MD)....................51
Catherine (Ledford) (NC).....77
Jane/Jean (Rowan) (PA)......39
John (NC)....................77

Robert (PA)...................2

David (DEL)..................44

Alexander John (SC).........88
Anna (SC).....................88
Ben (SC)......................87
Francis (Stribling) (SC)......89
George (SC)...................87
James (SC)....................87
Janet (Ross) (SC).............88
Jesse (SC)....................88

Alexander (KY, OH)..........99
Andrew (NC)...............77
Barbara (?) (NC).............80
James (NC)...................77
Jeremiah (VA)...............65
Margaret (Shed) (KY, OH)..99

David (PA)...................39

Caesar (VA)..................61
Ellen (VA)....................70
Fortune (SC)..................86
Henry (MD)...................48
Jenny (VA)....................63
Lucky (VA)...................62

Buckhanan
William (NC)..........................81
John (PA)..............................39
Thomas (SC, TN)..................88-89
Widow (PA)...........................41
William (PA)..........................40

Buckhanen

Buckhanin

Buckhannan
John (SC).............................88
John, Jr. (SC)........................88
Mary (SC)............................88
Mary (Wood) (SC)..................87
Micajah (SC).........................88
Susannah (SC)........................88
William (SC).......................88-89

Buckhannon
Samuel (NC).......................79-80
Sarah (VA)............................60
Sarah (Paschall) (NC)...............78
William (KY, OH)...................99
William (NC)......................78, 80

Buckhanon
Robert (NC)...........................79

Slaves
Paul (ARK, VA).......................69
Paul (VA)..............................70
Pete (VA)..............................70
Poll (ARK, VA)........................69
Sall (VA)...............................70
Sampson (ARK, VA)..................69

Slaves of William Buchaneneus (MD)...51

111

People Named Other than Buchanan

www.ingramcontent.com/pod-product-compliance
Lightning Source LLC
Chambersburg PA
CBHW072201270326
41930CB00011B/2506